MALAYALAM SELF-TAUGHT

MALAYALAM SELF-TAUGHT

BY THE NATURAL METHOD
WITH
PHONETIC PRONUNCIATION
(THIMM'S SYSTEM)

M. DE ZILVA WICKREMASINGHE

T. N. MENON

SECOND EDITION

GYAN

Published by

Gyan Publishing House
5, Ansari Road
Daryaganj, New Delhi-110002
Phone: 011-47034999, 9811692060
E-mail: books@gyanbooks.com

Distribution Network
gyanbooks.com
India, USA, Canada, UK, Australia, France

ISBN : 978-81-212-3741-3 (PB)
First Published,

2nd Impression 2020

Printed at: Gyan Press, Delhi.

Malayalam Self-taught
Author: M. De Zilva Wickremasinghe; T. N. Menon

Marlborough's Self-Taught Series.

Malayalam Self-Taught

by the Natural Method

WITH

Phonetic Pronunciation

THIMM'S SYSTEM

BY

Don M. de ZILVA WICKREMASINGHE

AND

T. N. MENON, B.A., Dip. Ec. (Madras)

SECOND EDITION

Revised and Enlarged by

T. N. MENON, B.A., Dip. Ec. (Madras)

PRINTED IN GREAT BRITAIN

LONDON:

E. MARLBOROUGH & Co., Ltd,

PREFACE.

In discharging the gratifying duty of revising the text for the SECOND EDITION, the writer has kept in mind certain lessons learnt in the course of instructing would-be learners of the language of the type contemplated when the book was first written. The result has been the incorporation in the present edition of conclusions arrived at after some intensive analysis, which, the writer claims, cannot be found in similar books on the subject.

The rules of euphony enumerated on pp. 77-81 are not put forward as either perfect, complete, or scientific, but are put forward as indispensable from a practical point of view, one of the first difficulties that assail a would-be learner being the mystery of the " y " or the " v " in " taṭa-y-um " or " taṭə-v-um." English-speaking people require no explanation of the " r " often heard in " India-r-office," or " saw-r-us," but if the words were pronounced (and worse, written) " India-v-office " or " saw-v-us," it would take them a minute or two to piece out the meaning.

The conjugation of Malayāḷam verbs has not yet been thoroughly gone into, the primary cause of confusion having been due to the fact that modern grammarians have either been groping pioneers like Dr Gundert, or Sanskrit-obsessed pundits. The first attempt at scientific analysis carried out to any satisfactory extent has been that of the late Raja Raja Varma.

It is regretted that the scope of the present volume does not allow of a scientific analysis of the verbs of the language, but it is confidently claimed that the indigenous roots, which are, in spite of 90 per cent. Sanskritization, the backbone of the language, have nowhere else, to my knowledge, been collected in such a convenient form for reference.

The tonic accent referred to on page 20 of the present edition was found to be more a source of confusion in the section on grammar than a help; this was because accents had to be employed both in transliteration (s′) and in phonetic pronunciation (n′, k′, t′, etc.). This has accordingly been deleted from the present edition.

The use of diacritical marks may be described as a deplorable necessity in transliterating Indian languages. In spite of careful proof-reading, a number of errors perforce crept into the first edition. These, it is hoped, have now been rectified.

T. N. MENON.

Aldwych, London, W.C.2,
January 1932.

PREFACE.

Malayāḷam is one of the Dravidian vernaculars spoken by about eleven million people, inhabiting the British District of Malabar and the Native States of Cochin and Travancore, on the south-western corner of India.

Owing to the comparatively recent, but rapid exploitation of the natural resources of this fertile tract, and to the ever-increasing field for evangelistic, educational, and commercial activities, there has been a growing demand for a manual of Malayāḷam, which would be useful for those who wish to acquire quickly a working knowledge of the language.

This, and the reception that has been accorded to the manuals in Tamil and Sinhalese in the same " Self-Taught " series, has encouraged us in compiling the present volume, incorporating, as in " Sinhalese Self-taught," an elementary outline of the Grammar.

Having regard to the needs of students who work without a teacher, we have devoted some pages wholly to the subject of pronunciation, and have given the transliteration of all the Malayāḷam words occurring in the grammar section of the work, side by side with the Malayāḷam character.

In the scheme of transliteration we have used full-faced type to mark the aspirate, instead of attaching the usual " h " to the aspirated consonant, on the principle of " one sign for one sound ": e.g.:— k, and **k** not kh.

As to the proper intonation of Malayāḷam words, we need only say that they follow those of the other Dravidian languages in having an even accent, though in practice a slight stress, due to pronouncing the initial syllable more fully and openly, is noticeable.

Moreover, in the sections containing the transliterated vocabularies and conversations, the correct pronunciation of every Malayāḷam word is indicated in the third column of each page by means of Marlborough's system of English phonetics.

This work being designed purely for practical use, the rules and explanations given in the grammar section are scracely intended for students entering on a scientific investigation of the Malayāḷam language.

M. de Z. WICKREMASINGHE.
T. N. MENON.

London, December 1926.

CONTENTS.

MALAYALAM SELF-TAUGHT.

THE ALPHABET AND PRONUNCIATION.

The modern Malayāḷam alphabet contains fifty-two letters; viz. sixteen vowels and thirty-six consonants

From these are formed 576 syllabic characters, which are combinations of the consonants with the vowels, in which the consonantal character is in some cases slightly modified in form and has a vowel-sign attached to it. To these must be added the Anusvāra and the Visarga, making a total of 578 characters.

Strictly speaking only five primary vowel-sounds in the Malayāḷam language are recognised by Malayāḷam grammarians. They are a, i, u, e, o. Each of these, however, is represented by two characters which stand for the long and the short sound of the vowel respectively, and there are in addition six characters representing (1) the Sanskrit letters ऋ ṛ, ॠ ṝ, ऌ ḷ, ॡ ḹ, and (2) the diphthongs ai and au. There are thus sixteen characters in the modern Malayāḷam alphabet which stands for vowel sounds. These are used in two different ways, that is to say,

(a) Initially, when they are denoted by separate letters;

(b) Medially, or following and joined to a consonant to form a syllable, when the vowel is represented by a sign (in certain instances variable) attached to the consonantal character, excepting in the case of the vowel *a*, which is inherent in the consonant and not indicated by any sign. Its absence in the case of k, ṇ, n, r, l, ḷ, is indicated by the vertical stroke (ɭ), thus:—ൿ, ൺ, ൻ, ർ, ൽ, ൾ. In all cases, the sign ᵕ placed on the top right-hand side of each letter shows that the inherent *a* is very slightly pronounced or is totally absent.

In the following tables, pp. 9-12, the initial and medial forms of the Malayāḷam vowels are given, followed by the consonants, and to all are added their transliterative Roman characters and the English phonetic signs by which the Malayāḷam sounds are represented throughout the classified vocabularies and conversations of which this volume mainly consists.

On pp. 14-19 are the syllabic characters also in the Malayāḷam and Roman types. These are preceded on p. 13 by some important compound consonants (with transliteration) where the consonantal signs have undergone modification.

1. Vowels or svaraṅṅal.

Malayalam chars. Initial.	Medial.	Trans-literation.	Pronunciation.	English Phonetic Signs.*
അ		a	Like *u* in *cut, bun.* In certain places, like *a* in *can.* Sometimes like *o* in *fodder* (approx.)	u a ȧ
	്	ȧ	Like *e* in *other, filbert,* when not forming the initial syllable of a word.	ŭ
ആ	ാ	ā	„ *a* in *father, car.*	*ah*
ഇ	ി	i	„ *i* or *y* in *pity, city.*	i
ഈ	ീ	ī	„ *i* in *routine* or *ee* in *meet*	ee
ഉ	ു	u	„ *u* in *put,* or *oo* in *good*	ŏŏ
ഊ	ൂ	ū	„ *u* in *rule,* or *oo* in *fool.*	oo
ഋ	ൃ	ṛ	Something like *ri* in *crick.*	ṛ
ൠ	ൄ	ṝ	The same sound lengthened	ṝ
ഌ	ൢ	ḷ	Something like *li* in *clip.*	ḷ
ൡ	ൣ	ḹ	The same sound lengthened.	ḹ
എ	െ	e	Like *e* in *egg, elbow.*	e
ഏ	േ	ē	„ *a* in *able.*	*ay*
ഐ	ൈ	ai	„ *i* in *mine,* or *I.*	i
ഒ	ൊ	o	„ *o* in *pot.*	o
ഓ	ോ	ō	„ *o* in *noble*	oh
ഔ	ൌ	au	„ *ow* in *now, cow.*	ow

* The notes on pronunciation on pp. 20 serve to emphasise the distinctive character of the phonetic signs.

2. Consonants or vyañjanaṅṅaḷ.

Malayalam Characters.	Trans-literation.	Pronunciation.	English Phonetic Signs.
ക്, ൿ	k	Initially or when doubled or in combination with other consonants (excepting s) like *k* in *kite*. Elsewhere, soft, midway between *k* and *g*.	k k′
ഖ്	**k**	Like *ckh* in *Lockhart* (approximately), i.e. an aspirated *k*.	**k**
ഗ്	g	,, *g* in *regard*.	g
ഘ്	**g**	,, *gh* in *foghorn* (approx.). i.e. an aspirated *g*.	**g**
ങ്	ṅ	,, *ng* in *song*.	ng
ച്	c	Initially or when doubled or in combination with other consonants, like *ch* in *church*. Elsewhere, soft, midway between *c* and *j*.	ch ch′
ഛ്	**c**	Like *chh* in *churchhouse* (approx.). i.e. an aspirated *ch*.	**ch**
ജ്	j	,, *j* in *jam*.	j
ഝ്	**j**	,, an aspirated *j* sound	**j**
ഞ്	ñ	,, gn in *cognac* (the Spanish ñ).	*ny*
ട്	ṭ	Initially or when doubled or in combination with other consonants, like *t* in *two* approx.). Elsewhere, soft, midway between ṭ and ḍ.	t t′
ഠ	**ṭ**	Like *th* in *pot-herb* (approx.), i.e. an aspirated ṭ sound.	**t**
ഡ്	ḍ	,, *d* in *door*.	d
ഢ്	**ḍ**	Like *dh* in *adhere* (approx.). i.e. an aspirated ḍ sound.	**d**

Malayalam Characters.	Trans-literation.	Pronunciation.	English Phonetic Signs.*
ണ് ൺ	ṇ	Cerebral *n* uttered with the tip of the tongue turned up and drawn back so as to touch the roof of the palate. Approximately like *n* in *hunting*.	*n*
ത്, ൽ	t	Like *th* in *with*, *thermometer*, if initial or doubled.	th
		Soft, midway between *t* and *d*.	th
		In combination with a following consonant sometimes like *l*, e.g. vatsan (pron. wulsun).	l
ഥ്	**t**	Aspirated *t* sound.	**th**
ദ്	d	Like *th* in *these*.	th
ധ്	**d**	Aspirated *d* sound.	*th*
ന്, ൻ	n	Initially, and sometimes when doubled, like the English *n*, uttered with the tongue in position as for *t* (a dental *n*).	n'
		Elsewhere as in English, e.g. *not*.	n
പ്	p	Like *p* in *pot*, when initial, doubled or in combination with other consonants.	p
		Elsewhere, soft, midway between *p* and *b*.	p
ഫ്	p	Aspirated *p* sound, approximately like *ph* in *shepherd*.	p
ബ്	b	Like *b* in *but*.	b
ഭ്	**b**	Aspirated *b* sound, approximately like *bh* in *abhor*.	b
മ്	m	As in English, e.g. *must*.	m
യ്	y	" " e.g. *yet*.	y

Malayalam Characters	Trans-literation.	Pronunciation.	English Phonetic Signs.
ര്, ർ	r	A very soft *r*, pronounced with the tip of the tongue, very slightly trilled against the upper gums.	r
ല്	l	As in English, e.g. *love*. Like ḷ in combination with preceding hard consonant.	l *l*
വ്	v	Midway between English *v* and *w*.	w
ശ്	ś	Palatal, having a sound between *s* and *sh*.	*s*
ഷ്	ṣ	Like *sh* in *cushion*.	sh
സ്	s	,, *s* in *sister*.	s
ഹ്	h	As in English.	h
ള്, ൾ	ḷ	Cerebral *l*, pronounced by turning up the tip of the tongue so as to touch the roof of the palate.	*l*
റ്, ർ	ṛ	Well trilled *r* like *r* in *rough* (approx.). Like *t* in *mint*, in combination with *n* preceding. Like *t* in *pit* *tt* in *betting*, when doubled	ṛ ṭ ṭṭ
ഴ്	ṟ	Cerebral *r*, pronounced by turning up the tip of the tongue almost to touch the roof of the palate.	ṟ
ം	m	Nasal, varying its pronunciation to suit the following consonant.	ṇg, *ny*, n', m
ഃ	h	Like *ch* in *loch* (Scottish *ch*).	ch

COMPOUND LETTERS.

Compound letters are in most cases written one above the other, the top letter being pronounced first; e.g.:— ഗ്ഗ gga, പ്ത pta, സ്മ sma. A few, however, are written side by side; e.g.:—ക്ത kta, ക്ഷ kṣa, ത്ത tta, മ്മ mma.

In others, the consonants undergo the following changes :—

(1) final യ ya becomes ്യ; e.g.:— ക്യ kya, ജ്യ jya; with the exception of double ya, which is written യ്യ yyà.

(2) ര r, റ ṟ, become ൎ when initial; e.g.:— ൎക്ക rkka, ൎഹ rha; and ്ര when final; e.g.:— ബ്ര bra, ശ്ര śṟa, ക്ര kṟa.

(3) final ല la becomes ്ല, and is pronounced ള ḷ, especially when preceded by a hard consonant; e.g.:— ക്ല kḷa, മ്ല mḷa, ബ്ല bḷa.

(4) final വ va becomes ്വ, when affixed; e.g.:— ക്വ kva, ശ്വ śva, ജ്വ jva; with the exception of double va, which is written വ്വ vva.

In addition to these there are the following compounds of somewhat irregular formation :—

ക്ക	ങ്ങ	ച്ച	ഞ്ഞ	ട്ട	ഡ്ഡ	ന്ന	ബ്ബ	ങ്ക	ഞ്ച	ണ്ട
kka	ṅṅa	cca	ñña	ṭṭa	dda	nna	bba	ṅka	ñca	ṇṭa
ന്ത	മ്പ	ണ്ക	ഞ്ജ	ത്ന	ഗ്ദ	ഗ്ന	ഗ്മ	ജ്ഞ	ന്ദ	
nta	mpa	ṇka	ñja	tna	gda	gna	gma	jña	nda	

ൎയ്യ, ൎയ ന്മ ദ്ദ

rya nma dda

The following table shows how the sixteen medial-
consonants, thereby producing

Consonants.	Absence of virama = a	ā	i	ī	u	ū	ṛ	ṝ
ക്,കം	ക	കാ	കി	കീ	കു	കൂ	കൃ	കൄ
k	ka	kā	ki	kī	ku	kū	kṛ	kṝ
ഖം	ഖ	ഖാ	ഖി	ഖീ	ഖു	ഖൂ	ഖൃ	ഖൄ
k	ka	kā	ki	kī	ku	kū	kṛ	kṝ
ഗം	ഗ	ഗാ	ഗി	ഗീ	ഗു	ഗൂ	ഗൃ	ഗൄ
g	ga	gā	gi	gi	gu	gū	gṛ	gṝ
ഘം	ഘ	ഘാ	ഘി	ഘീ	ഘു	ഘൂ	ഘൃ	ഘൄ
g	ga	gā	gi	gi	gu	gū	gṛ	gṝ
ങം	ങ	ങാ	ങി	ങീ	ങു	ങൂ	ങൃ	ങൄ
ṅ	ṅa	ṅā	ṅi	ṅi	ṅu	ṅū	ṅṛ	ṅṝ
ചം	ച	ചാ	ചി	ചീ	ചു	ചൂ	ചൃ	ചൄ
c	ca	cā	ci	ci	cu	cū	cṛ	cṝ
ഛം	ഛ	ഛാ	ഛി	ഛീ	ഛു	ഛൂ	ഛൃ	ഛൄ
c	ca	cā	ci	cī	cu	cū	cṛ	cṝ
ജം	ജ	ജാ	ജി	ജീ	ജു	ജൂ	ജൃ	ജൄ
j	ja	jā	ji	jī	ju	jū	jṛ	jṝ
ഝം	ഝ	ഝാ	ഝി	ഝീ	ഝു	ഝൂ	ഝൃ	ഝൄ
j	ja	jā	ji	jī	ju	jū	jṛ	jṝ
ഞം	ഞ	ഞാ	ഞി	ഞീ	ഞു	ഞൂ	ഞൃ	ഞൄ
ñ	ña	ñā	ñi	ñī	ñu	ñū	ñṛ	ñṝ
ടം	ട	ടാ	ടി	ടീ	ടു	ടൂ	ടൃ	ടൄ
ṭ	ṭa	ṭā	ṭi	ṭī	ṭu	ṭū	ṭṛ	ṭṝ
ഠം	ഠ	ഠാ	ഠി	ഠീ	ഠു	ഠൂ	ഠൃ	ഠൄ
ṭ	ṭa	ṭā	ṭi	ṭī	ṭu	ṭū	ṭṛ	ṭṝ

vowel signs are attached to the foregoing thirty-six 576 syllabic characters.

ḷ	ḹ	e	ē	ai	o	ō	au	Consonants.
കൢ	കൣ	കെ	കേ	കൈ	കൊ	കോ	കൌ	ക്, ൿ
kḷ	kḹ	ke	kē	kai	ko	kō	kau	k
ഖൢ	ഖൣ	ഖെ	ഖേ	ഖൈ	ഖൊ	ഖോ	ഖൌ	ഖ്
kḷ	kḹ	ke	kē	kai	go	kō	kau	k
ഗൢ	ഗൣ	ഗെ	ഗേ	ഗൈ	ഗൊ	ഗോ	ഗൌ	ഗ്
gḷ	gḹ	ge	gē	gai	go	gō	gau	g
ഘൢ	ഘൣ	ഘെ	ഘേ	ഘൈ	ഘൊ	ഘോ	ഘൌ	ഘ്
gḷ	gḹ	ge	gē	gai	go	gō	gau	g
ങൢ	ങൣ	ങെ	ങേ	ങൈ	ങൊ	ങോ	ങൌ	ങ്
ṅḷ	ṅḹ	ṅe	ṅē	ṅai	ṅo	ṅō	ṅau	n
ചൢ	ചൣ	ചെ	ചേ	ചൈ	ചൊ	ചോ	ചൌ	ച്
cḷ	cḹ	ce	cē	cai	co	cō	cau	c
ഛൢ	ഛൣ	ഛെ	ഛേ	ഛൈ	ഛൊ	ഛോ	ഛൌ	ഛ്
cḷ	cḹ	ce	cē	cai	co	cō	cau	c
ജൢ	ജൣ	ജെ	ജേ	ജൈ	ജൊ	ജോ	ജൌ	ജ്
jḷ	jḹ	je	jē	jai	jo	jo	jau	j
ഝൢ	ഝൣ	ഝെ	ഝേ	ഝൈ	ഝൊ	ഝോ	ഝൌ	ഝ്
jḷ	jḹ	je	jē	jai	jo	jō	jau	j
ഞൢ	ഞൣ	ഞെ	ഞേ	ഞൈ	ഞൊ	ഞോ	ഞൌ	ഞ്
ñḷ	ñḹ	ñe	ñē	ñai	ñō	ñō	ñau	ñ
ടൢ	ടൣ	ടെ	ടേ	ടൈ	ടൊ	ടോ	ടൌ	ട്
ṭḷ	ṭḹ	ṭe	ṭē	ṭai	ṭo	ṭō	ṭau	ṭ
ഠൢ	ഠൣ	ഠെ	ഠേ	ഠൈ	ഠൊ	ഠോ	ഠൌ	ഠ്
ṭḷ	ṭḹ	ṭe	ṭē	ṭai	ṭo	ṭō	ṭau	ṭ

Consonants.	Absence of virama = a	ā	i	ī	u	ū	ṛ	ṝ
ഡം	ഡ	ഡാ	ഡി	ഡീ	ഡു	ഡൂ	ഡൃ	ഡൄ
ḍ	ḍa	ḍā	ḍi	ḍī	ḍu	ḍū	ḍṛ	ḍṝ
ഢം	ഢ	ഢാ	ഢി	ഢീ	ഢു	ഢൂ	ഢൃ	ഢൄ
ḍ	ḍa	ḍā	ḍi	ḍī	ḍu	ḍū	ḍṛ	ḍṝ
ണ്, ൺ	ണ	ണാ	ണി	ണീ	ണു	ണൂ	ണൃ	ണൄ
ṇ	ṇa	ṇā	ṇi	ṇī	ṇu	ṇū	ṇṛ	ṇṝ
തം, ൽ	ത	താ	തി	തീ	തു	തൂ	തൃ	തൄ
t	ta	tā	ti	tī	tu	tū	tṛ	tṝ
ഥം	ഥ	ഥാ	ഥി	ഥീ	ഥു	ഥൂ	ഥൃ	ഥൄ
t	ta	tā	ti	tī	tu	tū	tṛ	tṝ
ദം	ദ	ദാ	ദി	ദീ	ദു	ദൂ	ദൃ	ദൄ
d	da	dā	di	dī	du	dū	dṛ	dṝ
ധം	ധ	ധാ	ധി	ധീ	ധു	ധൂ	ധൃ	ധൄ
d	da	dā	di	dī	du	dū	dṛ	d
നം, ൻ	ന	നാ	നി	നീ	നു	നൂ	നൃ	നൄ
n	na	nā	ni	nī	nu	nū	nṛ	nṝ
പം	പ	പാ	പി	പീ	പു	പൂ	പൃ	പൄ
p	pa	pā	pi	pī	pu	pū	pṛ	pṝ
ഫം	ഫ	ഫാ	ഫി	ഫീ	ഫു	ഫൂ	ഫൃ	ഫൄ
p	pa	pā	pi	pi	pu	pū	pṛ	pṝ
ബം	ബ	ബാ	ബി	ബീ	ബു	ബൂ	ബൃ	ബൄ
b	ba	bā	bi	bī	bu	bū	bṛ	bï
ഭം	ഭ	ഭാ	ഭി	ഭീ	ഭു	ഭൂ	ഭൃ	ഭൄ
b	ba	bā	bi	pī	bu	bū	bṛ	bṝ

ḷ	ḹ	e	ē	ai	o	ō	au	Consonants.
ഡൢ	ഡൣ	ഡെ	ഡേ	ഡൈ	ഡൊ	ഡോ	ഡൌ	ഡ്
ḍḷ	ḍḹ	ḍe	ḍē	ḍai	ḍo	ḍō	ḍau	ḍ
ഢൢ	ഢൣ	ഢെ	ഢേ	ഢൈ	ഢൊ	ഢോ	ഢൌ	ഢ്
ḍḷ	ḍḹ	ḍe	ḍē	ḍai	ḍo	ḍō	ḍau	ḍ
ണൢ	ണൣ	ണെ	ണേ	ണൈ	ണൊ	ണോ	ണൌ	ണ്
ṇḷ	ṇḹ	ṇe	ṇē	ṅai	ṇo	ṇō	ṇau	ṅ
തൢ	തൣ	തെ	തേ	തൈ	തൊ	തോ	തൌ	ത്
tḷ	tḹ	te	tē	tai	to	tō	tau	t
ഥൢ	ഥൣ	ഥെ	ഥേ	ഥൈ	ഥൊ	ഥോ	ഥൌ	ഥ്
tḷ	tḹ	te	tē	tai	to	tō	tau	t
ദൢ	ദൣ	ദെ	ദേ	ദൈ	ദൊ	ദോ	ദൌ	ദ്
dḷ	dḹ	de	de	dai	do	dō	dau	d
ധൢ	ധൣ	ധെ	ധേ	ധൈ	ധൊ	ധോ	ധൌ	ധ്
dḷ	dḹ	de	dē	dai	do	dō	dau	ḋ
നൢ	നൣ	നെ	നേ	നൈ	നൊ	നോ	നൌ	ന്
nḷ	nḹ	ne	nē	nai	no	nō	nau	n
പൢ	പൣ	പെ	പേ	പൈ	പൊ	പോ	പൌ	പ്
pḷ	pḹ	pe	pē	pai	po	pō	pau	p
ഫൢ	ഫൣ	ഫെ	ഫേ	ഫൈ	ഫൊ	ഫോ	ഫൌ	ഫ്
pḷ	pḹ	pe	pē	pai	po	pō	pau	p
ബൢ	ബൣ	ബെ	ബേ	ബൈ	ബൊ	ബോ	ബൌ	ബ്
bḷ	bḹ	be	bē	bai	bo	bō	bau	b
ഭൢ	ഭൣ	ഭെ	ഭേ	ഭൈ	ഭൊ	ഭോ	ഭൌ	ഭ്
bḷ	bḹ	be	bē	bai	bo	bō	bau	b

Consonants.	Absence of virama = a	ā	i	ī	u	ū	r̥	r̥̄
മ്	മ	മാ	മി	മീ	മു	മൂ	മൃ	മൄ
m	ma	mā	mi	mī	mu	mū	mr̥	mr̥̄
യ്	യ	യാ	യി	യീ	യു	യൂ	യൃ	യൄ
y	ya	yā	yi	yī	yu	yū	yr̥	yr̥̄
ര്, ർ	ര	രാ	രി	രീ	രു	രൂ	രൃ	രൄ
r	ra	rā	ri	rī	ru	rū	rr̥	rr̥̄
ല്	ല	ലാ	ലി	ലീ	ലു	ലൂ	ലൃ	ലൄ
l	la	lā	li	lī	lu	lū	lr̥	lr̥̄
വ്	വ	വാ	വി	വീ	വു	വൂ	വൃ	വൄ
	va	vā	vi	vī	vu	vū	vr̥	vr̥̄
ശ	ശ	ശാ	ശി	ശീ	ശു	ശൂ	ശൃ	ശൄ
ś	śa	śā	śi	śī	śu	śū	śr̥	śr̥̄
ഷ്	ഷ	ഷാ	ഷി	ഷീ	ഷു	ഷൂ	ഷൃ	ഷൄ
ṣ	ṣa	ṣā	ṣi	ṣī	ṣu	ṣū	ṣr̥	ṣr̥̄
സ്	സ	സാ	സി	സീ	സു	സൂ	സൃ	സൄ
s	sa	sā	si	sī	su	sū	sr̥	sr̥̄
ഹ്	ഹ	ഹാ	ഹി	ഹീ	ഹു	ഹൂ	ഹൃ	ഹൄ
h	ha	hā	hi	hī	hu	hū	hr̥	hr̥̄
ള്	ള	ളാ	ളി	ളീ	ളു	ളൂ	ളൃ	ളൄ
ḷ	ḷa	ḷā	ḷi	ḷī	ḷu	ḷū	ḷr̥	ḷr̥̄
റ്	റ	റാ	റി	റീ	റു	റൂ	റൃ	റൄ
ṟ	ṟa	ṟā	ṟi	ṟī	ṟu	ṟū	ḷr̥	ḷr̥̄
ഴ്	ഴ	ഴാ	ഴി	ഴീ	ഴു	ഴൂ	ഴൃ	ഴൄ
ṛ	ṛa	ṛā	ṛi	ṛī	ṛu	ṛū	ṛr̥	ṛr̥̄

ḷ	ḹ	e	ē	ai	o	ō	au	Consonants.
മൢ	മൣ	മെ	മേ	മൈ	മൊ	മോ	മൌ	മ്
mḷ	mḹ	me	mē	mai	mo	mō	mau	m
യൢ	യൣ	യെ	യേ	യൈ	യൊ	യോ	യൌ	യ്
yḷ	yḹ	ye	yē	yai	yo	yō	yau	y
രൢ	രൣ	രെ	രേ	രൈ	രൊ	രോ	രൌ	ര്
rḷ	rḹ	re	rē	rai	ro	rō	rau	r
ലൢ	ലൣ	ലെ	ലേ	ലൈ	ലൊ	ലോ	ലൌ	ല്
lḷ	lḹ	le	lē	lai	lo	lō	lau	l
വൢ	വൣ	വെ	വേ	വൈ	വൊ	വോ	വൌ	വ്
vḷ	vḹ	ve	vē	vai	vo	vō	vau	v
ശൢ	ശൣ	ശെ	ശേ	ശൈ	ശൊ	ശോ	ശൌ	ശ്
śḷ	śḹ	śe	śē	śai	śo	śō	śau	ś
ഷൢ	ഷൣ	ഷെ	ഷേ	ഷൈ	ഷൊ	ഷോ	ഷൌ	ഷ്
ṣḷ	ṣḹ	ṣe	ṣē	ṣai	ṣo	ṣō	ṣau	ṣ
സൢ	സൣ	സെ	സേ	സൈ	സൊ	സോ	സൌ	സ്
sḷ	sḹ	se	sē	sai	so	sō	sau	s
ഹൢ	ഹൣ	ഹെ	ഹേ	ഹൈ	ഹൊ	ഹോ	ഹൌ	ഹ്
hḷ	hḹ	he	hē	hai	ho	hō	hau	h
ളൢ	ളൣ	ളെ	ളേ	ളൈ	ളൊ	ളോ	ളൌ	ള്
ḷḷ	ḷḹ	ḷe	ḷē	ḷai	ḷo	ḷō	ḷau	ḷ
റൢ	റൣ	റെ	റേ	റൈ	റൊ	റോ	റൌ	റ്
ṛḷ	ṛḹ	ṛe	ṛē	ṛai	ṛo	ṛō	ṛau	ṛ
ഴൢ	ഴൣ	ഴെ	ഴേ	ഴൈ	ഴൊ	ഴോ	ഴൌ	ഴ്
ṛḷ	ṛḹ	ṛe	ṛē	ṛai	ṛo	ṛō	ṛau	ṛ

PRONUNCIATION.

The student is recommended to master the pronunciation at the outset. The precise use and value of each phonetic sign are shown on pp. 9-12, which should be carefully studied. The following additional explanations will be of service.

The principles on which Marlborough's system of phonetics is based are: (1) the employment of English characters with their ordinary pronunciation (or one of their sounds, where more than one) with as sparing a use as possible of diacritical signs; and (2) one sign, one sound. Where, therefore, a 'sign' (i.e. letter or letters) might be variously sounded—and this applies to each of the English vowels and some of the consonants—its particular use in the scheme of phonetics should be carefully noted, and each sign must always be sounded in the same manner wherever it occurs (one sign, one sound); any letter or combination of letters printed in distinctive type (italics, etc.) or with any mark added has a special use which must be learnt.

TONIC ACCENT.

It should be noticed that the first syllable of a Malayāḷam word, as a general rule, has a fuller intonation than the remaining syllables of the word.

VOCABULARIES.

The World and its Elements.

(Lōkavum, Pañcabūtaṅṅaḷum)

English.	Malayalam.	Pronunciation.
Air	vāyu	w*ah*yo͝o
cloud	mēgam	m*ay*gum
cold	taṇuppȧ	thu*n*o͝oppŭ
darkness	iruṭṭȧ	iro͝ottŭ
dew	maññȧ	mu*nyny*ŭ
earth	būmi	boomi
East	kiṛakkȧ	kiṛakkŭ
fire	tiyyȧ, tī, agni	thiyyŭ, thee, ugn'i
fog	mūṭal-maññȧ	moot'al-mu*nyny*ŭ
hail	āli-p-paṛam	*ah*li-p-puṛam
heat	cūtȧ, uṣṇam	choot'ŭ, o͝osh*n*am
light	veḷiccam	we*l*ichcham
lightning	minnal	minnal
moon	candran	chun'*th*ran
moonlight	nilāvȧ	n'il*ah*wŭ
nature	pṛakṛti	pṛak'*r*th'i
North	vaṭakkȧ	wut'akkŭ
rain	maṛa	muṛu
rainbow	maṛa-villȧ	muṛu-willŭ
shade	taṇalȧ [mbam	thu*n*alŭ [mbum
shadow, reflection	niṛalȧ, pṛatibi-	n'iṛulŭ, pṛath'ibi-
sky	ākāśam	*ah*k'*ah*sam
South	tekkȧ	thekkŭ
sun	sūryan	sooryan
thunder	iṭi	it'i
water	veḷḷam	we*ll*am
West	paṭiññāṛȧ	put'i*nynyah*ṛŭ
wind	kāṟṟȧ	k*ah*ṯṯŭ

Land and Water.
(Karayum Veḷḷavum).

English.	Malayalam.	Pronunciation.
Bank (of a river or	kara, tīram	kuru, theeram
backwater [lake)	kāyalǎ	k*ah*yalŭ
coast	kaṭalōram	kut'al*oh*ram
foam	pata, nura	puth'u, n'ōōru
hill	kunnǎ	kōōn'n'ŭ
ice	kaṭṭa-maññǎ	kuttu-mu*nyny*ŭ
island	turuttǎ	thōōrōōththŭ
lake	taṭākam	thut'*ah*k'um
land	kara	kuru
mountain	mala	mulu
mud	caḷi	chu*l*i
plain	maitānam	m*i*th'*ah*nam
pond	kuḷam	kōō*l*am
river	puṛa, nadi, āṟǎ	pōōṛu, n'u*th*i, *ah*ṟŭ
rock	pāṟa	p*ah*ṟu
sand	maṇalǎ	mu*n*alŭ
sea	kaṭalǎ	kut'alŭ
shore	kara, tīram	kuru, theerum
star	nakshatram	n'uk'shathṟum
storm	koṭum-kāṟṟǎ	kot'ōōṉg-k'*ah*ṯṯŭ
stream	aruvi, cōla	urōōwi, ch*oh*lu
tank	kuḷam	kōō*l*am [ṯum
tide (high)	ēṟṟam, vēliyēṟṟam	*ay*ṯṯam, w*ay*liy*ay*ṯ-
,, (low)	iṟakkam, vēliyiṟak-	iṟakkum, w*ay*liyi-
valley	tāṟvara [kam	th*ah*ṟwuru [ṟakkum
water (fresh)	nalla veḷḷam	n'ullu we*ll*am
,, (salt)	uppu-veḷḷam	ōōppŭ-we*ll*am
waterfall	veḷḷa-c-cāṭṭum	we*ll*u-ch-ch*ah*ttum
wave	ala, tira	ulu, thiru
well	kiṇaṟǎ	ki*n*aṟŭ

Minerals and Metals (Lōhādikaḷ).

Brass	piccaḷa	pichcha*l*u
bronze	ōṭǎ, veḷḷōṭǎ	*oh*t'ŭ, we*lloh*t'ŭ

English.	Malayalam.	Pronunciation.
cement	śīma-k-kummāyam	seemuk-kŏŏmm*ah*-yam
chalk	śīma-nūṟȧ	seemu-n'ooṟŭ
clay	kaḷimaṇṇȧ	ku*l*imu*nn*ŭ
coal	kal-k-kari	kulkkuri
copper	cempȧ	chemp'ŭ
coral	paviṟam	puwiṟam
diamond	vairam	wiram
emerald	maratakam	muruth'uk'um
glass	cillȧ, kuppi	chillŭ, kŏŏppi
gold	svarṇam, ponnȧ, taṅkam	swuṟnam, ponnŭ, thuṉgk'um
granite	karińkallȧ	kuriṉgk'ullŭ
sand	maṇalȧ	mu*n*alŭ
gravel	caralȧ	churalŭ
iron	irumpȧ	irŏŏmp'ŭ
laterite	ceṅkallȧ	cheṉgk'ullŭ
lead	īyam	eeyam
lime (unslaked)	ittiḷȧ	iththi*l*ŭ
„ (slaked)	nūṟȧ, cuṇṇāmpȧ	nooṟŭ, chŏŏ*nnah*-mp'ŭ
marble	veḷḷakkallȧ, veṇkal-lȧ	we*ll*ukkullŭ, weṉg-k'ullŭ
mercury	rasam	rasum
pearl	muttȧ, nanmuttȧ	mŏŏththŭ, n'un-mŏŏththŭ
plumbago	kāriyam	k*ah*reeyam
ruby	māṇikyam	m*ahn*ikyam
sapphire	indranīlam	in'*th*run'eelum
silver	veḷḷi	we*ll*i
soda	śīmac-cāram	seemuch-ch*ah*ram
steel	urukkȧ	ŏŏrŏŏkkŭ
stone	kallȧ	kullŭ
tin	takaram	thuk'arum
zinc	tuttanākam	thŏŏththun*ah*k'um

Animals, Birds, Fishes and Insects

(Mṛgam, pakṣi, matsyam, jantu mutalāyava).

Animal	pṟāṇi	pṟ*ahn*i
ant	uṟumpȧ	ŏŏṟŏŏm'p'ŭ

English.	Malayalam.	Pronunciation.
barking	kurakkal	kŏŏrakkul
bear	karaṭi	kurat'i
beast	mṛgam	m*r*gum
bird	pakṣi	puk'shi
bleating	karaccil	kurachchil [kul
braying	karaccil, cinakkal	kurachchil, chinak-
bull	kāḷa, mūri	k*ahl*u, moori [wŭ
calf	kannȧ, paikkiṭāvȧ	kun'n'ŭ, p*i*kkit'*ah*-
cat	pūcca	poochchu
cattle	nālkkāli	n'*ah*lkk*ah*li
cock	pūvaṇkōṛi	poowaṉgk'*oh*ṛi
cow	paśu, paiyyȧ	pusŏŏ, p*i*yyŭ
crab	ñaṇṭȧ	*nyun*t'ŭ
crow	kākka	k*ah*kku
dog	paṭṭi, nāya	putti, n'*ah*yu
donkey	kaṛuta	kuṛŏŏth'u
duck	tāṛāvȧ	th*ah*ṛ*ah*wŭ
eagle	kaṛukan	kuṛŏŏk'an
eel	āral	*ah*ral
elephant	āna	*ah*nu
feather	tūval	thoowal
fish	matsyam	mulsyam
fowl	kōṛi [nari	k*oh*ṛi [ṛŏŏnuri
fox	kuṛukkan, kuṛu-	kŏŏṛŏŏkkun, kŏŏ-
goat	kōlāṭȧ	k*oh*l*ah*t'ŭ
he-goat	koṟṟaṉ	koṯṯan
goose	vattȧ	wuththŭ
hair	rōmam	r*oh*mum
hare	muyalȧ	mŏŏyalŭ
hen	piṭa-k-kōṛi	pit'a-k-k*oh*ṛi
herd	kūṭṭam	koottum
hoof	kuḷampȧ	kŏŏ*l*amp'ŭ
horn	kompȧ	komp'ŭ
horse	kutira	kŏŏth'iru
lamb	āṭṭinkuṭṭi	*ah*ttiṉgkŏŏtti
lion	simham	simhum

English.	Malayalam.	Pronunciation.
mane	kuñcumuṭi, kuñci-rōmam	kōōnych'ŭmoot'i, kōōnych'irohmum
monkey	kuraṅṅan	kōōrangngan
mosquito	kotu	koth'ōō
mouse	cuṇṭeli	chōōnt'eli
mule	kōvaṟ-kaṟuta	kohwaṟ-kuṟōōth'u
mongoose	kīri	keeri
neighing	cinakkal	chinakkal
owl	mūṅṅa, kūman	moongngu, kooman
ox	mūri, kāḷa	moori, kahlu
oysters	cippimīn	chippimeen
parrot	tatta	thuththu
paw	kaippatti	ki-p-puththi
peafowl	mayil	muyil
peahen	mayil-pēṭa	muyil-payt'u
pig	panni, pōṟkkă	pun'n'i, pohṟkkŭ
pigeon	pṟāvȧ	pṟahwŭ
prawn	cemmīn	chemmeen
quail	kāṭa	kaht'u
rat	eli	eli
salt-fish	uppu-mīn	ōōppŭ-meen
dried-fish	uṇakka-mīn	ōōnakku-meen
salmon	kuyil-mīn, kuḷavan	kōōyil-meen, kōōla-wun
salt-pan or pit	uppaḷam	ōōppulam
shark	sṟāvȧ	sṟahwŭ
sheep	āṭȧ, cemmariyāṭȧ	aht'ŭ, chemmari-yaht'ŭ
shrimp	ceḷḷi, koñcȧ, cem-mīn	chelli, konych'ŭ, chemmeen
silk-worm	paṭṭunūlpuṟu	puttŭn'oolpōōṟōō
snake	pāmpȧ	pahmp'ŭ
snipe	puḷḷȧ, mūṟakkan, kōṭṭān	pōōllŭ, mooṟakkun, kohttahn
sparrow	kurikil, aṟakkiḷi, kūri	koorik'il, uṟakkili koori
spider	eṭṭukāli, cilanti	ettōōk'ahli, chilun'th'i
squirrel	aṇṇān, aṇṇārak-kaṇṇan	unnahn, unnahrak-kunnan
stork	kokkȧ, koṟṟi	kokkŭ, koṭṭi

English.	Malayalam.	Pronunciation.
swallow	mīval	meewal
swan	arayannam	ŭruyannum
tail	vālă	w*ah*lŭ
teal	iraṇṭa	iru*n*t'u
tiger	nari, puli	n'uri, pŏŏli
trout	pūmīn	poomeen [kum
turkey	vāṇkōri, kalkkam	w*ah*ṉgk'*oh*ṛi, kulk-
turtle (tortoise)	āma	a*h*mu
vulture	rājāḷi	r*ah*j*ahl*i
whiting	noṅṅal, pūṛān	n'oṉgṉgal, pooṛ*ah*n
wing	ciṛakă	chiṛak'ŭ
wolf	cennāya	chen'n'*ah*yu
wood-pecker	maram-kotti	muraṉgk'oththi
wood-pigeon	kāṭṭu-pṛāvă	k*ah*ttŭ-p'ṛ*ah*wŭ
sole (fish)	mantală, noṅkămīn	mun'thalŭ, n'oṉg-k'ŭmeen

Trees, Fruits, Flowers, Vegetables, &c.

(Maraṅṅaḷ, paṛaṅṅaḷ, pūkkaḷ, sasyaṅṅaḷ, mutalāyava).

Apple (wood-)	viḷāmpaṛam, bḷa-ṅkāya	wi*lah*mpuṛam, b*lah*-ṉgk'*ah*yu
,, (custard-)	ātta-c-cakka	*ah*ththu-ch-chukku
,, (jujube-)	ḷantappaṛam	lun'th'uppuṛam
,, (rose-)	panīr-c-cāmpakka	puneeṛ-ch-ch*ah*m-p'akku
banana	nēntṛap--paṛam	n'*ay*n'th'ṛappuṛam
bark	tōlă, paṭṭa [ka	th*oh*lŭ, puttu [kụ
beans	amaṛakka, avarak-	umurakku, uwurak-
,, , French	acciṅṅa, maṇippa-yaṛă	uchchiṉgṉgu, mu*n*ippayaṛŭ
bouquet	pūccenṭă	poochche*n*t'ŭ
branch	kompă	komp'ŭ
cabbage	moṭṭakkūs	mottukkoos
cauliflower	pūkkūs	pookkoos
chilli	muḷakă	mŏŏ*l*ak'ŭ
cinnamon	ilavaṛṅam	ilawuṛṉgum

English.	Malayalam.	Pronunciation.
cloves	karayāmpūvȧ	kurayahmp'oowŭ
cocoanut	nāḷikēram, tēṅṅa	n'ahlikayram, thay-ngngu
„ , tender	iḷanīr, karikkȧ	ilan'eer, kurikkŭ
cocoanut palm	teṅṅȧ	thengngŭ
cucumber	veḷḷarikka	wellarikku
ebony	karimaram, kariṅ-	kurimuram, kuring-
fern	panna [ṅāli	punnu [ngahli
fig	atti-p-paḻam	uththi-p-puram
fig-tree	atti	uththi
banian-tree	ālȧ	ahlŭ
fir-tree	devatāram	thaywuth'ahram
flower	pū, puvvȧ	poo, poowwŭ
garlic	veḷuttuḷḷi	weloo̅ththoo̅lli
ginger	iñci	inych'i
„ (dry)	cukkȧ	choo̅kkŭ
grapes	muntiriṅṅa	moo̅n'th'iringngu
kernel	kaṟumpȧ, parippȧ	kuroo̅mp'ŭ, purippu
leaf	ila	ilu
lemon	nāraṅṅa	n'ahrangngu
lily (water-)	āmpal	ahmp'al
lime	ceṟu-nāraṅṅa	cheroo̅-n'ahrangngu
lotus	tāmara	thahmuru
mace	jātipatri	jahth'ip'uthri
mango	māṅṅa	mahngngu
„ (ripe)	māmpaḻam	mahmp'uram
„ -tree	māvȧ	mahwŭ [muththan
melon	mattaṅṅa, mattan	muththangngŭ,
marrow (vegetable)	kumpaḷaṅṅa	koo̅mp'ulangngŭ
mulberry	amaṟātti	umarahththi
nut	aṇṭi [yaṇṭi	unt'i [ngk'iyunt'i
„ (cashew-)	kaśuvaṇṭi, paṟaṅki-	kusoo̅wunt'i, pura-
oak-tree	karuvēlakam	kuroo̅waylukʼum
olive	ōlīvȧ	ohleewŭ
opium	kaṟappȧ, apīn	kurappŭ, upeen
orange	madura-nāraṅṅa	muthooru-n'ahrang-
palmyra-palm	pana	punu [ngu

English.	Malayalam.	Pronunciation.
peas	payaṟa	puyaṟŭ
pepper	kurumuḷaka, nalla-muḷakȧ	kŏŏrŏŏmŏŏlak'ŭ, nullumŏŏlak'ŭ
pineapple	kaitaccakka	kith'a-ch-chukku
plantain (ripe)	paṟam	puṟam
„ (unripe)	vāṟakka	wahṟakku
plum	pḷampaṟam	plum-p'uṟam
pomegranate	mātaḷa-nāraṅṅa	mahth'alu-n'ahrangnguu
poppy	avīn-ceṭi, kaskkas-ceṭi	uween-ch'eṭ'i, kusk-kus-ch'et'i
potatoes	uruḷa-k-kiṟaṅṅȧ	ŏŏrŏŏla-k-kiṟangngŭ
rape seed	eḷḷȧ	ellŭ
reed	ññāṅṅaṉa	nyahngngunu
root	vērȧ, kiṟaṅṅȧ	wayrŭ, kiṟangngŭ
rose	ṟōsā-p-pūvȧ	ṟohsah-p-poowŭ
saffron	maññaḷ	munynyal
sago	sāgōri	sahgohri
tea-leaf	cāya, tēyila	chahyu', thayyilu
tea (beverage)	cāya	chahyu,
teak	tēkkȧ	thaykkŭ
tobacco	pukayila	pŏŏk'ayilu
tomato	takkāḷi	thukkahli
tree-trunk	kātal	kahth'al
turnip	muḷḷaṅki	mŏŏllangk'i
vine	muntiri-vaḷḷi	mŏŏn'th'iri-wulli
water-melon	kummaṭṭikka	kŏŏmmuttikku

Colours (Niṟaṅṅaḷ).

Black, dark	karuppȧ	kuṟŏŏppŭ
blue	nīla	n'eelu
brown	taviṭṭȧ	thuwittŭ
crimson	kaṭum-cuvappȧ	kut'ŏŏm-ch'ŏŏwappŭ
green	pacca	puchchu
grey	cāraniṟam	chahrun'iṟam
light (pale)	viḷaṟiya-niṟam	wiluṟiyu-n'iṟum
orange	lagu-maññа	lugŏŏ-munynyu

English.	Malayalam.	Pronunciation.
pink	ilañcuvappå	ilanycch'ŏowappŭ
purple	indra-nīlam	in'thru-n'eelam
red	cuvappå, cumappå	chŏowappŭ, chŏo-
violet	ūta	ooth'u [mappŭ
white	veḷuppå	welŏoppŭ
yellow	maññа	munynyu

Times and Seasons (Kāla-ṛtukkaḷ):

Afternoon	ucca-tiriññå nēram	ŏochchuth'irinynyu
birthday	piṟannāḷ	piṟan'n'ahl [n'ayram
Christmas	valiya perunnāḷ	wuliyu perŏon'n'ahl
date	tiyyati	thiyyuth'i
dawn	veḷuppān-kālam, prabātam	welŏoppahn-k'ahlum, prubahth'am
day	divasam, nāḷå	thiwasum, n'ahlŭ
day-time	pakalå	puk'alŭ
day, to	innå	in'n'ŭ
days of the week	ārcakaḷ	ahṛch'uk'ul
Sunday	ñāyaṟārca	nyahyaṟahṛch'u
Monday	tiṅkaḷārca	th'ingk'ulahṛch'u
Tuesday	covvārca	chowwahṛch'u
Wednesday	budanārca	bŏothanahṛch'u
Thursday	vyārārca	wyahṛahṛch'u
Friday	veḷḷiyārca	welliyahṛch'u
Saturday	śaniyārca	saniyahṛch'u
Easter	uyirēṟṟa-p-perunnāḷ	ŏoyiraytṯu-p-perŏon'n'ahl
evening	vaikunnēram	wik'oon'n'ayram
fortnight	pakṣam	puk'sham
Good Friday	duka veḷḷiyārca	thooku welliyahṛch'u
holiday	oṛivu-divasam, muṭakkadivasam	oṛiwŭ-thiwasum, mŏot'akkuthiwasum
day of the full moon	veḷutta vāvå	welŏoththu wahwŭ
„ new moon	karutta vāvå	kuṟŏoththu wahwŭ

English.	Malayalam.	Pronunciation.
hour [minutes	maṇikkūṟ	munikkooṟ
,, (Indian) 24	nāṟika	n'ahṟiku [rahthṟi
midnight	pātira, aṟdarātṟi	pahth'iru, urthu-
midsummer	naṭu-vēnal	n'ut'ōō-waynal
minute	miniṭṭȧ, nimiṣam	minittŭ, n'imisham
month	māsam	mahsum
month by month	māsam tōṟum, māsam pṟati	mahsam thohṟōōm, mahsam pṟath'i
monthly payment (wages)	māsappaṭi	mahsupput'i
,, (salary)	śampaḷam	sump'ulam
months, the	māsaṅṅal	mahsuṉgṉgul
August-Sept.	ciṅṅam	chiṉgṉgam
September-Oct.	kanni	kunni
October-Nov.	tulām	thōōlahm
November-Dec.	vṛścikam	wrsch'ik'am
December-Jan.	danu	thunōō
January-Feb.	makaram	muk'urum
February-March	kumbam	kōōmbum
March-April	mīnam	meenam
April-May	mēṭam	mayt'am
May-June	iṭavam	it'awum
June-July	mitunam	mithōōnam
July-August	kaṟkkiṭakam	kuṟkkit'ak'um
morning	kālattȧ, rāvile	kahlaththŭ, rahwile
this morning	innu kālattȧ, innu rāvile	in'n'ŭ kahlaththŭ, in'n'ŭ rahwile
tomorrow	nāḷe	n'ahle
,, (day-after-)	maṟṟannāḷ	muṭṭan'n'ahl
twilight	sandya, anti	sun'thyu, un'th'i
night	rātṟi	rahthṟi
noon	ucca, naṭṭucca	ōōchchu, n'uttōōchchu
Seasons, the	ṛtukkaḷ	ṛth'ōōkkul
Spring	vasantakālam	wusun'th'u kahlam
Summer	grīṣmakālam, vēnalkkālam	greeshmu kahlam, waynalkkahlam
Autumn	śaralkkālam	suralkkahlam
Winter	hēmanta kālam	haymun'th'u kahlam

English.	Malayalam.	Pronunciation.
Rainy Season, the	varṣakkālam, varṣam	wurshukk*ah*lam, wursham
Rainless " "	vēnalkkālam, vēnal	*wa*ynalkk*ah*lam, *wa*ynal
second (time)	ñoṭiyiṭa, mātṟa	*ny*ot'iyit'u, m*ah*thṟu
sunrise	udayam	ŏŏ*th*ayum
sunset	astamanam	usthumnunam
week	āṟca	*ah*ṟch'u
year	kollam, āṇṭá	kollam, *ahn*t'ŭ
century	nūṟṟāṇṭá	n'ooṯṯ*ahn*t'ŭ
yesterday	innale	in'n'ale

Town and Country (Nagaravum Nāṭṭupuṟavum).

Bridge	pālam	p*ah*lam
bush	kuṟṟikkāṭa, kuṟuṅkāṭá	kŏŏṯṯikk*ah*t'ŭ, kŏŏṟŏŏṉgk'*ah*t'ŭ
cathedral	metṟan paḷḷi	methṟ*ah*n pu*ll*i
church	paḷḷi	pu*ll*i
country	nāṭá, dēśam, rājyam	n'*ah*t'ŭ, *thay*sam, r*ah*jyam
country-side	nāṭṭupuṟam	n*ah*ttŭpŏŏṟam
ditch	cālá, kāna, tōṭá	ch*ah*lŭ, k*ah*nu, th*oh*t'ŭ
farm	kaḷam, kṛṣi	ku*l*um, k*r*shi
farmhouse	kaḷa-p-pura	ku*l*u-p-pŏŏru
fence	vēli	w*ay*li
field	vayalá, kaṇṭam	wuyalŭ, ku*n*t'am
farmer	kṛsi-k-kāran	k*r*sh-ik-k*ah*ran
foot-path	kālvaṟi, caviṭṭuvaṟi	k*ah*lwuṟi, chuwittŭwuṟi
forest	kāṭá, vanam	k*ah*t'ŭ, wunam
gate	paṭi	put'i
grass	pullá	pŏŏllŭ
hut	kuṭilá	kŏŏt'ilŭ
inn	vaṟiyampalam	wuṟiyump'ulam
jungle	kāṭá	k*ah*t'ŭ
log	taṭi	thut'i
market	canta	chun'th'u
meadow	maitānam	m*i*th'*ah*nam
mile	nāṟika, mailsá	n*ah*ṟiku, m*i*lsŭ

English.	Malayalam.	Pronunciation.
mill	cakkả	chukkŭ
mill-stone	tirukallả	thiro͝ok'ullŭ [bum
monument	smāraka stambam	sm*ah*rak'u-sth'um-
palace	kōvilakam, koṭṭā-	k*oh*wiluk'um, kott*ah*-
road	pāta, vaṛi [ram	p*ah*th'u, wuṛi [rum
lane	iṭavaṛi	it'uwuṛi
school	eṛuttupaḷḷi. paḷḷi-kkūṭam	eṛo͝oththŭp'u*ll*i, pu*l*-*l*ikkoot'um
shepherd	āṭṭiṭayan	*ah*ttit'ayun
shop	pīṭika, pāṇṭyāla, ṣāppả	peet'ik'u, p*ahn*t'y*ah*-lu, sh*ah*ppŭ
coffee-shop, café	kāppi-k kaṭa, kāp-pi hōttel	k*ah*ppi-k-kut'u, k*ah*ppi h*oh*ttel
square	caturam	chuth'o͝oram
stile	kaṭampa	kut'amp'u
straw	vaikkōl	w*i*kk*oh*l
street	teruvả	thero͝owŭ [thṛam
temple	ampalam, kṣetṛam	ump'alum, k'sh*ay*-
town	paṭṭaṇum	putta*n*um
university	saṛvakalāśāla	suṛwukul*ahsah*lu
village	grāmam	gr*ah*mum

Mankind ; Relations. (Manuṣya-jāti ; Sambandikaḷ).

Aunt ; mother-in-	ammāyi	umm*ah*yi
brother (elder) [law	cēṭṭan ; ēṭṭan	ch*ay*ttan ; *ay*ttan
— (younger)	aniyan	uniyan [nan
— in-law	aḷiyan, maccunan	u*l*iyan, muchcho͝o-
daughter	makaḷ	muk'a*l*
father	accan	uchchan
—'s elder brother	valiyaccan	wuliyuchchan
—'s young brother	iḷayaccan ; cheṛia-ccan	i*l*ayuchchan ; cheri-yuchchan
grandfather	muttaccan	mooththuchchan
grandmother	muttaśśi	mo͝ot'hthussi
great grandfather	appūppan	uppooppan
great grandmother	ammūmma	ummoommu

English.	Malayalam.	Pronunciation.
husband	baṟttavă	buṟthth*ah*wŭ
man	manuṣyan, āḷă	munŏŏshyan ; *ahlŭ*
male	āṇă	*ahn*ŭ
mother's brother	ammāman	umm*ah*man
„ sister	ciṟṟamma ; ciṟṟaś-śi ; iḷayamma, ceṟiyamma	chiṭṭummu ; chiṭ-ṭ*ussi* ; *il*ayummu ; cheṟiyummu
nephew (sister's son) ; son-in-law	marumakan	murŏŏmuk'an
niece (sister's daughter) ; daughter in-law	marumakaḷ	murŏŏmuk'a*l*
sister (elder)	ēṭatti, cēcci, ōppa	*ay*t'aththi ; ch*ay*ch-chi ; *oh*ppu
„ (younger,	anītti ; aniyatti	uneeththi ; uniyath-thi
sister	peṅṅaḷ	peṉgṉgu*l*
brother	āṅṅaḷă	*ah*ṉgṉgu*l*u
son	makan	muk'an
stepmother	maṟṟamma	muṭṭammu
old man	kiṛavan, tanta	kiṛawun ; thun'thu
old woman	kiṛavi, taḷḷa	kiṛawi, thu*ll*u
widow	vidava	wi*th*awu
wife	bārya	b*ah*ryu
woman	stṟī, peṇṇă	sthṟee, pe*nn*ŭ

The Human Body (Mānuṣa—śarīram).

Ankle	kaṇaṅkāl, kaṇṇak-kāl	ku*n*aṉgk'*ah*l ; ku*n*-*n*ukk*ah*l
arm	kaiyyă	k*i*yyŭ
armpit	kakṣam	kuk'sham
back	puṟam, mutukă	pŏŏṟam, mŏŏth'ŏŏ-k'ŭ
beard	tāṭi	th*ah*t'i
blood	cōra	ch*oh*ru
body	dēham ; śarīram	*thay*hum ; sureeram
bone	ellă	ellŭ
bowels	kuṭală	kŏŏtalŭ
brain	tala-c-cōṟa	thula-ch-ch*oh*ṟŭ
brains (intelli-gence)	buddi	bŏŏ*thth*i

English.	Malayalam.	Pronunciation.
breast, chest	māṟȧ, neññȧ	m*ah*ṟŭ ; n'*enyny*ŭ
cheek	kaviḷȧ	kuwi*l*ŭ
chin	tāṭi	th*ah*ṭ'i
complexion	niṟam	n'iṟum
ear	kātȧ, cevi	k*ah*th'ŭ, chewi
elbow	kaimuṭṭȧ	k*i*mŏŏttŭ
eye	kaṇṇȧ	ku*nn*ŭ
eye-brow	purikam, piriyam	pŏŏrik'um ; piriyam
eye-lid	kaṇ-pōḷa	ku*n*-p'*oh**l*u
face	mukam	mŏŏkum
finger	viral	wiral
foot	aṭi, kālaṭi	ut'i, k*ah*lut'i
forehead	neṟṟi	neṯṯi [mum
hair	talamuṭi, rōmam	thulumŏŏt'i ; roh-
hand, palm	kaiyyȧ ; kaippa-ṭam ; kaippatti	k*i*yyŭ ; k*i*pput'am ; k*i*ppuththi
head	tala	thulu [*ah*wŭ
„ (crown of)	śirassȧ, mūṟddāvȧ	sirassŭ, mooṟ*thth*-
heart	hṛdayam [āṇi	h*rth*ayum
heel	uppu-kuṟṟi, neri-y-	ŏŏppŭ-k'ŏŏṯṯi, n'eri-
hip	iṭuppȧ	it'ŏŏppŭ [y*ah*ni
jaw	tāṭa	th*ah*t'u
knee	muṭṭȧ	mŏŏttŭ
leg	kālȧ	k*ah*lŭ
lip	cuṇṭȧ	chŏŏ*n*t'ŭ
liver	karaḷȧ, īṟalȧ	kura*l*ŭ, eeṟalŭ
lung	śvāsakōśam	swahsak'*oh*sam
moustache	mīśa	meesu
mouth	vāya, vāy	w*ah*yu, w*ah*y
nail	nakam	n'ukam
neck	kaṟuttȧ	kuṟŏŏththŭ
nose	mūkkȧ	mookkŭ
rib	vāri-y-ellȧ	w*ah*ri-y-ellŭ
shoulder	tōḷȧ, cumal	th*oh**l*ŭ, choomal
side	bāgam	b*ah*gam
skull	tala-y-ōṭȧ	thulu-y-*oh*t'ŭ
spine	naṭṭellȧ	n'uttellŭ

English.	Malayalam.	Pronunciation.
stomach	vayaṟȧ	wuyaṟŭ
temple	karaṇam	kuru*n*am
throat	toṇṭa	tho*n*t'u
thumb	taḷḷa-viral	thu*ll*u-wiral
tongue	nāvȧ, nākkȧ	n'*ah*wŭ, n'*ah*kkŭ
tooth	pallȧ	pullŭ
trunk (of the body)	uṭal	ŏŏt'al
wrist	maṇikkaṇṭam	mu*n*ikku*n*t'am
whiskers	kṛtāvȧ	k*r*th*ah*wŭ

Health (Dēhasukam, ārōgyam).

English.	Malayalam.	Pronunciation.
Accident	apakaṭam	up'uk'at'um
bandage	keṭṭȧ	kettŭ
bile	pittam	piththum
bite	kaṭi	kut'i
—, snake-	pāmpu-kaṭi	p*ah*mp'ŭ-k'ut'i
blindness	kaṇṇu-kāṇāyma, kuruṭattam	ku*nn*ŭ-k'*ahnah*ymu, kŏŏrŏŏt'uththum
blind man	kuruṭan	kŏŏrŏŏt'an
blister	pokkiḷa, poḷḷal	pokki*l*u, po*ll*al
bruise	catavȧ	chuth'awŭ
burn	poḷḷal	po*ll*al
Chemist's shop	marunnu-ṣāppȧ	murŏŏn'n'ŭ-sh*ah*ppŭ
chill	nīriḷakkam, jala-dōṣam	n'eeri*l*akkum, jalu-*thoh*shum
cholera	viṣūcika, talē-t-taṭṭi	wishŏŏch'ik'u, thu-*lay*ththutti
contagion	pakaṟcca	puk'aṟchchu
corns	āni	*ahn*i
cough	cuma, kura	c̆hoomu, kŏŏru
cramp	kōccal	k*oh*chchul
cure (for a disease)	pratividi	pruthiwi*th*i
,, (state of having been cured)	bēdam-ākal	b*ayth*am*ah*k'ul
deaf (man)	poṭṭan, cekiṭan	pottan, chek'it'an
dentist	danta-vaidyan	*th*un'th'u-wi*th*yan

English.	Malayalam.	Pronunciation.
diarrhœa	vayaṛṛiḷakkam	wuyaṭṭi*l*akkum
diet	pattyam	puth**th**yam
disease, illness	dīnam, rōgam	*th*eenam, r*oh*gam
doctor	dākkaṭṭaṛ	d*ah*kkuttaṛ
„ (native)	vaidyan	w*ith*yan
dose	mātṛa	m*ah*thṛu
dumb (man)	ūma, mūkan	oomu, mook'an
dysentery	cōra pōkkȧ, atisā-ram	ch*oh*ru p'*oh*kku, uth'is*ah*ram
exercise	vyāyāmam, āyā-sam	wy*ah*y*ah*mum, *ah*-y*ah*sam
faint (to)	mōhālasya-p-peṭu-ka	m*oh*h*ah*lasyu-p-pe-t'uk'u
fatigue	taḷaṛcca, kṣīṇam	thu*l*aṛchchu, k'shee-*n*am
fever	pani, jvaram	puni, jwarum
—, light	kāccil	k*ah*chchil
—, enteric	viṣa-j-jvaram	wishu-j-jwarum
—, of nights	rā-p-pani	r*ah*-p-puni
—, malarial	malampani	mulump'uni
fracture	uṭavȧ	oot'uwŭ
gout	vātam	w*ah*th'am
head-ache	tala-k-kuttȧ	thuluk-kooththŭ
illness, sickness	sukakkēṭȧ	sookukk*ay*t'ŭ
indigestion	dahana-k-kēṭȧ	*th*uhunuk-k*ay*t'ŭ
inflammation	paṛuppȧ	puṛooppŭ
lameness	muṭantȧ, noṇṭal	moot'un'th'ŭ, n'*on*-t'al
lame man	muṭantan, noṇṭi	moot'un'than, n'*on*-t'i
medicine	marunnȧ	muroon'n'ŭ
nurse	paricārika	purich'*ah*rik'u
ointment	kuṛampȧ	kooṛamp'ŭ
pain	vēdana, nōvȧ	w*ayth*anu, n'*oh*wŭ
paralysis	pakṣavātam	puk'shuw*ah*th'am
pill	guḷika	goo*l*ik'u
poison	viṣam, naññȧ	wisham, n'u*nyny*ŭ
poultice	pōṭṭisȧ	p*oh*tteesŭ
prescription	vidi, yōgam, ma-runnu-kuṛippȧ	wi*th*i, y*oh*gam, mu-roon'n'ŭ-kooṛippŭ

English.	Malayalam.	Pronunciation.
quinine	koyana	koyanu
remedy	parihāram	purih*ah*ram
scald	poḷḷal	po*ll*al
scratch (as of a thorn)	kīṟā	keeṟŭ
— („ an animal	māntā	m*ah*n'th'ŭ
sore	vṛṇam	w*r*nam
cut	muṟi	mo͝oṟi
sore-eyes	ceṅkaṇṇā	cheṉgk'u*nn*ŭ
sprain	uḷukkā	o͝o*l*o͝okkŭ
sting	kottā, kaṭi	koththŭ, kut'i
surgeon	śastṟa-vaidyan	susthṟu-w*ith*yan
small-pox	vasūri	wusoori
chicken pox	nīṟ-p-pōḷaṅ	n'eeṟ-p-p*oh*l*an
swelling	nīrā	n'eerŭ
boil	kuru, pōḷan	ko͝oro͝o, p*ohl*an
plague	mahāmāri, pḷēgā	muh*ah*m*ah*ri, p*lay*-gŭ
wound	muṟi	mo͝oṟi

Food and Drink (Bakṣaṇa—pānīyaṅṅaḷ).

Bacon	uppiṭṭ'-uṇakkiya pannimāmsam	o͝oppitt'o͝o*n*akkiyu pun'n'im*ah*msam
beef	paśu-māmsam	puso͝o-m*ah*msam
bottle	kuppi	ko͝oppi
bread	ṟoṭṭi, appam	ṟotti ; uppam
breakfast	pṟātal	pṟ*ah*th'al
butter	veṇṇa	we*nn*u
cake	palahāram, appam	pulah*ah*ram, uppam
cheese	pāl-k-kaṭṭi	p*ah*l-k-kutti
chocolate	cōkkaḷēṟṟā	ch*oh*kk*ulay*ṯṯŭ
claret	kḷāreṟṟā	k*lah*reṯṯŭ
coffee	kāppi, kappi	k*ah*ppi, kuppi
cream	pālāṭa	p*ahlah*t'u
curry	kūṭṭān, kaṟi	koott*ah*n, kuṟi
dinner	muttāṟam	mo͝othth*ah*ṟam
eggs	muṭṭa	mo͝ottu
fat	koṟupppā	koṟo͝oppŭ

English.	Malayalam.	Pronunciation.
fish	malsyam	mulsyam
flour	māvȧ	ma*h*wŭ
honey	tēn	th*ay*n
ice	maññu-kaṭṭa	mu*nyny*ŭ-k'uttu
jam	jām	ja*h*m
kidney	karaḷ	kura*l* [msam
lamb [made)	āṭṭiṅkuṭṭi māmsam	*ah*ttingk'ōōtti ma*h*-
lemonade (home	nāraṅṅā-b-bōñji	n'*ah*rangng*ah*-b-bo*h*-
„ (bottled)	lemaṅēdȧ	lema*nay*dŭ [*ny*ji
luncheon	eṭanēram, tipin	et'an'*ay*ram, tipin
meat	māmsam, iṟacci	m*ah*msam, iṟachchi
—, boiled	vēvicca māmsam	w*ay*wichchu ma*h*msam
—, roast	varaṭṭiya māmsam	wurattiyu ma*h*msam
milk	pālȧ	pa*h*lŭ
mustard	kaṭukȧ	kut'ōōk'ŭ
mutton	āṭṭin-māmsam	*ah*ttin-ma*h*msam
oil	eṇṇa	e*nn*u
onion	uḷḷi	ōō*ll*i [ōō*ll*i
— (Spanish)	sabōḷa, bōmbā uḷḷi	subo*hl*u, bo*h*mba*h*
— (shallots)	uḷḷi, cumannuḷḷi	ōō*ll*i,chōōman'n'ōō*ll*i
garlic	veḷuttuḷḷi	we*l*ōōththōō*ll*i
pepper	kurumuḷakȧ, nallamuḷakȧ	kōōrōōmōō*l*ak'ŭ, n'ullumōō*l*ak'ŭ
pork	pōṟkkȧ, pannimāmsam	po*h*ṟkkŭ, pun'n'i-ma*h*msam
port wine	pōṟṭṭa viññȧ, māssȧ viññȧ	po*h*ṟttŭ wee*nyny*ŭ, ma*h*ssŭ wee*nyny*ŭ
pudding	pāyasam, maduram	pa*h*yasum, mu*th*ōō-
rice	ari	uri [ram
—, boiled	cōṟȧ	cho*h*ṟŭ
—, cakes	aṭa	ut'u
salad	paccila-k-kaṟi	puchchilak-kuṟi
salt	uppȧ	ōōppŭ
sherry	ṣeṟi viññȧ	sheṟi wee*nyny*ŭ
soda-water	sōṭa	so*h*t'u
soup	sūppȧ, cāṟȧ	sooppŭ, cha*h*ṟŭ

English.	Malayalam.	Pronunciation.
stew	iṣṭu	isht'ōō
sugar	pañcasāra	punych'asahru
supper	attāṛam	uththahṛam
tea	cāya	chahyu
tobacco	pukayila	pōōk'ayilu
underdone	kuṛaccu mātṛam vēvicca	kōōṛachchŭ mahthṛam waywichchu
veal	paikkiṭāvin māmsam	pikkit'ahwin mahmsam
vegetable	kāykaṟi	kahykuṟi
—, (greens)	pacca-k-kaṟi	puchchu-k-kuṟi
venison	māniṟacci	mahniṟachchi
vinegar	curakka, vinākari	chōōrakku, winahk'uri
water	veḷḷam	weḷḷam
—, cold	pacca veḷḷam	puchchuweḷḷam
—, hot (boiled with dry ginger)	cukkuveḷḷam	chōōkkuweḷḷam
—, tepid	kāññavellam	kahnynyuweḷḷam
well done	nallavaṇṇam vēvicca	n'ulluwannum waywichchu
wine	vīñña, vīññȧ	weenynyu, weenynyŭ

Cooking and Eating utensils

(veppu-pātṛaṅṅaḷum, ūṇ-pātṛaṅṅaḷum).

Basin	uruḷi	ōōrōōli
bowl	kiṇṇam	kinnam
coffee-pot	kāppi-p-pātṛam	kahppi-p-pahthṛam
cork-screw	kuppi tuṛappa	kōōppi thōōṛappu
cruet-stand	veññana-t-taṭṭȧ	wenynyanu-th-thuttŭ
cup	kōppa, kappȧ	kohppu, kuppŭ
dish	piññāṇam	pinynyahnam
fork	muḷḷȧ	mōōllŭ
frying pan	cīna-c-caṭṭi, karaṇṭi	cheenachchutti, kurant'i
glass, (tumbler)	kḷāssȧ, tumbḷēṛȧ	klahssŭ, thumblayṛŭ
grill	irumpaṭuppȧ	irōōmp'ut'ōōppŭ
jar	baraṇi, iṭṭuruṭṭi	burani, ittōōrōōtti
kettle	keṭṭilȧ, kēttalȧ	keṭṭilŭ, kayththulŭ

English.	Malayalam.	Pronunciation.
knife	katti	kuththi
ladle	tavi, kuṛutal, kayil	thuwi, ko͞oṛo͞othal, kuyil
lid	mūṭī	moot'i
saucer	aṭi-k-kiṇṇam	ut'i-k-ki*nn*am
serviette	mēśa-t-tūvāla	m*ay*su-th-thoow*ah*lu
spoon	ceṟutavi, karaṇṭi	cheṟo͞oth'uwi, kurant'i
—, (dessert-)	ara-t-tuṭam, dessaṟṭṭu kuṛutal	uruththut'am, dessaṟttŭ ko͞oṛo͞oth'al
—, (table-)	tuṭam, tavi, mēśa-k-karaṇṭi	tho͞ot'am, thuwi, m*ay*sakkura*nt*'i
—, (tea-)	kāl tuṭam, cāy-k-karaṇṭi	k*ah*l tho͞ot'am, chaykkura*nt*'i
table-cloth	mēśa-t-tuṇi, mēśa viri	m*ay*suththo͞o*n*i, m*ay*suwiri
tea-pot	cāya-p-pātṟam	ch*ay*u-p-p*ah*thṟam
tray	taṭṭȧ	thuttŭ
wine-glass	vīññȧ-kḷāssȧ	wee*nyny*ŭ-k*lah*ssŭ

Dress and Dressing (Uṭuppu mutalāyava).

English.	Malayalam.	Pronunciation.
Boots	būṭṭīsȧ	bootteesu
boot-tree	accu kaṭṭa	uchchŭ kuttu
bracelet	kāppȧ, vaḷa	k*ah*ppŭ, wu*l*u
braces	cumalvāṟ	cho͞omalw*ah*ṟ
brush	bṟaṣṣȧ, tūppȧ	bṟushshŭ, thooppŭ
buttons	kuṭukki	ko͞ot'o͞okki
button-hook	kuṭukki-k-koḷuttȧ	ko͞ot'o͞okki-k-ko*l*o͞oththŭ
calico	cīṭṭi-t-tuṇi	cheetti-th-tho͞o*n*i
cap (cloth-)	toppi	thoppi
cloak, (cape)	kuppāyam	ko͞opp*ah*yam
cloth	tuṇi	tho͞o*n*i
clothes-brush	uṭuppu bṟaṣṣȧ	o͞ot'o͞oppŭ bṟushshŭ
coat	puṟaṅkuppāyam	po͞oṟangk'o͞opp*ah*yam
comb	cīṟppȧ, cīppȧ	cheeṟppŭ, cheeppŭ
cotton (thread)	parutti nūlȧ	puro͞oththi n'oolŭ

English.	Malayalam.	Pronunciation.
dress (clothing)	uṭuppȧ	ŏŏt'ŏŏppŭ
flannel	pḷānalȧ, pḷeyam	p*lah*nalŭ, p*l*eyam
gloves	kaiyyuṛa	k*i*yyŏŏṛu
handkerchief	uṛumal, kailēsȧ	ŏŏṛŏŏm*ahl*, k*ilay*sŭ
hair-pin	muṭisūci	mŏŏt'isooch'i
hat	toppi, caṭṭa-t-toppi caṭṭa	thoppi, chuttu-th-thoppi, chuttu
jewelery	paṇṭam, ābaraṇam	puṇt'am, *ah*bura*n*um
lace	kasavȧ, ṛēnta	kusawŭ, r*ay*n'th'u
linen	caṇanūl-t-tuni	chu*n*an'ool-th-thŏŏni
mirror	kaṇṇāṭi	ku*nnah*t'i
muslin	malamalȧ, mallȧ	mulamulŭ, mullŭ
necklace	patakkam, kaṇṭa-śaram	puth'akkum, ku*n*ta-suram
neck-tie	kaṛutti'-k-keṭṭȧ	kuṛŏŏththi'-k-kettŭ
needle	tūśi, sūci	thoosi, soochi
overcoat	mēlaṅki, mēl-k-kuppāyam	m*ay*luṇgk'i, m*ay*l-k-kŏŏpp*ah*yam
parasol	ceṛukuṭa	cheṛŏŏk'ŏŏt'u
pin	moṭṭutūśi	mottŭth'oosi
pocket	kīśa	keesu
purse	paṇa-s-sañci	pu*n*as-su*n*ych'i
razor	kṣaura-k-katti	k'sh*ow*rak-kuththi
ring (for finger)	mōtiram	m*oh*th'iram
scissors	kattira	kuththiru
shoes	ceruppȧ, pāppāssȧ	cherŏŏppŭ, p*ah*p-p*ah*ssŭ
sandals	muṭṭi-c-ceruppȧ	mŏŏtti-ch-cherŏŏppŭ
clogs	metiyaṭi	meth'iyat'i
shoe-lace	ceruppu-caraṭȧ	cherŏŏppŭ-churatŭ
silk	paṭṭȧ	puttŭ
soap	sōppȧ	s*oh*ppŭ
string	caraṭȧ	churat'ŭ
skirt	pāvāṭa	p*ah*w*ah*t'u
slippers	ceruppȧ	cherŏŏppŭ
thread	nūlȧ	n'oolŭ
tooth-brush	pal-bṛaṣṣȧ	pul-bṛushshŭ
trousers	kaḷasam, kāloṛa, ijār	ku*l*asum, k*ah*loṛu, ij*ah*r

English.	Malayalam.	Pronunciation.
umbrella	kuṭa	ko͝ot'u
veil	mūṭupaṭam	mo͝ot'ŭput'am
walking-stick	vaṭi	wut'i
watch	gaḍiyāḷ	gadiy*ahl* [yam
waterproof (coat)	maṟa-k-kuppāyam	muṟu-k-ko͝opp*ah*-
wool	kambḷi	kumb*li*

Washing List (Alakku—kaṇakkȧ).

Apron	muntuṇi	mo͝on'th'o͝o*ni*
bathing dress	kuḷi-y-uṭuppȧ	ko͝o*li*-y-o͝ot'o͝oppŭ
bed-clothes	viri, kacca	wiri, kuchchu
blanket	kampiḷi, putappȧ	kump'*ili*, po͝oth'appŭ
bodice	ṟavukka, jākkeṟṟȧ	ṟawo͝okku, j*ah*kkeṯ-
cap	toppi	thoppi [ṯŭ
chemise	kammīsȧ	kummeesŭ
collar	kaṟuttu-paṭṭa	kuṟo͝oththŭ-puttu
combinations	kāluṟa-k-kuppā-	k*ah*lo͝oṟu-k-ko͝opp*ah*-
coverlet	viri, kacca [yam	wiri, kuchchu [yam
cuff	kaippaṭṭa	k*i*pputtu
drawers	aṭi-k-kaḷasam	ut'i-k-ku*l*asum
dress (gown)	aṅki	uṉgk'i
handkerchief	uṟumāl, kailēsȧ	o͝oṟo͝om*ahl*, k*i*l*ay*sŭ
jacket	jākkeṟṟȧ	j*ah*kkeṯṯŭ
napkin	kaittūvāla	k*i*ththoow*ah*lu
necktie	kaṟutti'-k'-keṭṭȧ	kuṟo͝oththi'-k-kettŭ
nightdress	rātṟi-y-uṭuppȧ	r*ah*thṟi-y-o͝ot'o͝oppŭ
night-shirt	rātṟi-k-kuppāyam	r*ah*thṟi-k-ko͝opp*ah*-
pants	aṭi-k-kaḷasam	ut'i-k-ku*l*asum [yam
petticoat	uḷ-p-pāvāṭa	o͝o*l*-p-p*ah*w*ah*t'u
pillow-case	talēṇa-y-uṟa	thul*ayn*a-y-o͝oṟu
pinafore	muntuṇi	mo͝on'th'o͝o*ni*
pyjamas	pijāma	pij*ah*mu
serviette	mēśa-t-tūvāla	m*ay*suththoow*ah*lu
sheet	viri, kacca	wiri, kuchchu
shirt	aṭi-k-kuppāyam, kammīsȧ	ut'i-k-ko͝opp*ah*yam, kummeesŭ

English.	Malayalam.	Pronunciation.
socks	mē'-j-jōṭȧ	may'-j-joht'ŭ
stays	kaccȧ	kuchchŭ
stockings	valiya mē-j-jōṭȧ	wuliyu may'j-joht'ŭ
table cloth	mēśaviri, mēśat-tuṇi	maysu-wiri, maysu-th-thooni
towel	tūvāla, tōṟttȧ	thoowahlu, thohṟth-thŭ
trousers	kālkkuṭukki, kā-luṟa	kahlkkoot'ookki, kahlooṟa
	kaḷasam, ijāṟ	kulasum, ijahṟ
undervest	baniyan	buniyan
vest	vesṟṟu kuppāyam	westṭŭ-kooppahyam

House and Furniture (vīṭum, vīṭṭu sāmānaṅṅaḷum).

Ante-room	naṭappura	n'ut'appooru
arm chair	kaiyuḷḷa kasāla	kiyoollu kusahlu
basket	kuṭṭa, vaṭṭi	koottu, wutti
bed	kiṭakka, kōsaṭi	kit'akku, kohsat'i
bed-room	kiṭakka-y-aṟa, kiṭ-appu-muṟi	kitakku-y-uṟu, kit'-appŭ-mooṟi
blind (window)	janēri-t-tira	junayri-th-thiru
book-case	pustaka alumāri	poosth'uk'u uloom-ahri
box	peṭṭi	petti
broom	cūlȧ	choolŭ
candle	meṛutiri	meṛooth'iri
candlestick	meṛutiri-t-tattȧ	meṛoothiri-th-thut-[tŭ
carpet	paravadāni	purawuthahni
chair	kasāla, kasēri	kusahlu, kusayri
chamber utensils	kitappumuṟi sāmā-naṅṅaḷ	kit'appŭ-mooṟi sah-mahnangngul
chest of drawers	valippalumāri	wulippuloomahri
chimney	pukakkuṛal, cim-mini	pook'u-k-kooṛal, chimmini
closet	maṟappura, kakkū-sȧ	muṟuppooru, kuk-koosŭ

English.	Malayalam.	Pronunciation.
clock	maṇi, gaṭikāram	muni, gat'ik'ahram
couch	kavicci, metta	kuwichchi, meththu
cupboard	cumar-alumāri	choomar-uloomahri
curtain	tiraśśila, maṟa	thirasseelu, muṟu [lu
„ (window)	janēri-t-tiraśśila	junayri-th-thirassee-
cushion	metta, cārutalēṇa	meththu, chahrūth' ulaynu
dining room	ūṭṭupura, agraśāla	oottūpooru, ugra-sahlu
door	vātil, kataka	wahthil, kuth'ak'ū
door-bell (street)	teruvȧ-vātil-maṇi	theroowū-wahth'il-muni
drawing room	virunnu-muṟi, salk-kāramuṟi	wiroon'n'ū-mooṟi, sulkkahrumooṟi
easy chair	cārukasāla	chahroo-kusahlu
electric light	vidyuccakti veḷic-cam	withyoochchuk'thi welichcham
fender	tī-t-taṅṅi	theeththahṅgṅgi
fire	tiyyȧ, tī	thiyyū, thee
fire place	aṭuppȧ	ut'ooppū
floor	nilam, taṟa	n'ilam, thuṟu
garden	tōṭṭam	thohttum [yoo
gas	kattikkum vāyu	kuththikkoom wah-
grate	tīkrāti	theekrahth'i
hall (entrance)	taḷam	thulam
key	tākkōlȧ	thahkkohlū
kitchen	aṭukkaḷa, kus'ini	ut'ookkulu, koosini
„ dresser	kus'ini-mēs'a	koosini-maysu
lam	viḷakkȧ	wilakkū
larder	iṟacci-y-alumāri	iṟachchi-y-uloomahri
library	grantȧ-ppura, pu-staka-s'āla	grun'thuppooru, poosthuku-sahlu
plock	pūṭṭȧ	poottū
looking-glass	kaṇṇaṭi	kunnaht'i
piano	ṣaṃgīta-p-peṭṭi	sumgeeth'u-p-petti
picture	citṟam, paṭam	chithṟam, put'am
pillow	talēṇa	thulaynu

English.	Malayalam.	Pronunciation.
poker	ti-y-iḷakki	theeyi*l*akki
roof	mēlppura	m*ay*lppōōru
room	muṛi, aṛa, pura	mōōṛi, uṛu, pōōru
shelf	taṭṭȧ	thuttŭ
sideboard	cumarȧ-palaka	chōōmarŭ-pulaku
staircase	kōṇi-p-paṭi	k*oh*n*ipput'i
stairs	paṭikaḷ	put'ik'u*l*
table	mēśa	m*ay*su
table cover	mēśaviri	m*ay*suwiri
tiles	ōṭȧ	*oh*t'ŭ
tongs	cavaṇa	chuwu*n*u
vase, (flower-)	(pū-c-) caṭṭi	(poo-ch-) chutti
verandah	vṛānta	wṛ*ah*n'th'u
wall (of a house)	cumarȧ	chōōmarŭ
„ (outer)	matilȧ	muth'ilŭ
window	janēri, janāla kiḷi-vātil	jun*ay*ri, jun*ah*lu, ki*l*i-w*ah*thil

Professions and Trades (Toṛilukaḷ)

Architect	śilpāśāri	*s*ilp*ahsah*ri
artisan	kaittoṛilukāran	k*i*ththoṛilŭk'*ah*ran
baker	ṛoṭṭikkāran	ṛottikk*ah*ran
banker	uṇṭikakkāran	ōōnt'ik'ukk*ah*ran
barber	veḷakkattaravan, kṣaurakkāran, am-piṭṭan	we*l*ukkuththurawun k'sh*ow*rakk*ah*ran, ump'ittan
blacksmith	kollan, karuvān	kollan, kurōōw*ah*n
brazier	mūśāri	moo*sah*ri
bookseller	pustaka - k - kacca-[vaṭa-k-kāran	pōōsthuk'u-k-kuch[chawut'u-k-k*ah*ran
butcher	kaśāppukāran	ku*sah*ppŭ-k'*ah*ran
carpenter	āśāri	*ahsah*ri
chemist (druggist)	marunnu-ṣāppȧ-kāran	murōōnnŭsh*ah*ppŭ-k'*ah*ran
clergyman	pātiri, accan	p*ah*th'iri, uchchan
confectioner	miṭāyi-k-kāran	mit*ah*yikk*ah*ran

D

English.	Malayalam.	Pronunciation.
consul	pṟatinidi	pṟath'inithi
cook	veppukāran, kuśi-nikkāran	weppūk'ahran, kōō-sinikkahran
cycle maker	caviṭṭāvaṇṭi uṇ-ṭākkunnavan	chuwittūwunt'i ōōn-t'ahkkōōn'n'uwun
dentist	danta-vaidyan	thun'th'u-withyan
doctor	vaidyan, ḍākkaṭṭa-rā	withyan, dahkkattu-rū
engineer	iñcinīrā	inych'in'eerū
farrier	lāṭa-k-kollan	laht'ukkollan
„ (veterinary)	mṟgavaidyan	mrguwithyan
fruiterer	kāykani-k-kāran	kahyk'uni-k-kahran
fisherman (by caste)	mukkuvan	mōōkkōōwan
florist	pū-k-kāran	pookkahran
goldsmith	taṭṭān	thuttahn
grocer	palacarakkā kacca-vaṭakkāran	puluchurakkū kuch-chuwut'uk-kahran
hatter	toppi-y-unṭākkun-navan	thoppi-y-ōōnt'ahk-kōōn'n'uwun
ironmonger	irumpu kaccava-ṭakkāran	irōōmp'ū kuchchu-wut'ukkahran
jeweller	ābaraṇa-vyāpāri	ahbarunu-wyahpahri
laundress	veḷuttēṭatti	welōōththayt'aththi
merchant	kaccavaṭakkāran	kuchchuwut'ukkah-ran
miller	cakkān	chukkahn
milliner	stṟīvastṟa, vyāpāri	sthṟeewusthṟu wyah-pahri
money changer	paṇam māṟṟunna-van	punam mahṯṯōōnnu-wun
optician (seller)	kaṇṇaṭa-k-kacca-vaṭa-k-kāran	kunnut'u-k-kuch-chuwut'u-k-kahran
painter, decorator	cāyam tēkkunna-van	chahyam thayk-kōōn'n'uwun
photographer	cāya eṭukkunna-van	chahyu et'ōōkkōōn'-n'uwun
policeman	pōlisākāran	pohleesūkahran
porter (carrier)	cumaṭṭu-kūlikkā-ran	chōōmuttū-kooli-k-kahran

English.	Malayalam.	Pronunciation.
postmaster	tappal-māsṛṛarå	thuppahl-mahsṭṭurŭ
printer	accaṭikkāran	uchchut'ik-kahran
saddler	kutira-k-kōppå uṇ-[ṭakkunnavan	kooth'irukkohppŭ oont'ahkkoonnuwun
schoolmaster	aśān, vaddyārå	ahsahn, wahththyah-rŭ
servant	vāliyakkāran	wahliyuk-kahran
shoemaker	tōl-k-kollan, cerup-pu kutti	thohl-k-kollan, che-rooppŭ kooththi
shopkeeper	pīṭika-k-kāran	peet'ik'ukkahran
singer (vocalist)	bāgavatar	bahgawuthur
smith	kollan	kollan
soldier	paṭayāḷi	put'ayahli
student	vidyaṛtti	withyahṛththi
surgeon	śastṛa vaidyan	susthṛu withyan
surveyor (land)	saṛvēkkāran	suṛwaykkahran
tailor	tunna'k-kāran	thoonnu'k-kahran
teacher	guru	gooroo
tobacconist	pukayila-k-kāran	pook'ayiluk-kahran
tradesman	kaccavaṭakkāran	kuchchuwut'ukkah-ran
washerman	veḷutteṭan, vaṇ-ṇān, ḍōbi	welooththayt'an, wunnahn, dohbi
watchmaker	maṇi-y-uṇṭākkun-navan	muni-y-oont'ahk-koon'n'uwun

Travelling (sañcarikkal).

Arrival	varavå	wurawŭ
arrive, to	vannu cēruka	wun'n'oo chayrook'u
bag	sañci	sunych'i
bill	kaṇakkå	kunakkŭ
box, trunk	peṭṭi	petti
bridle	kaṭiññāṇ	kut'inynyahn
cabman	vaṇṭikkāran, kuti-rakkāran	wunt'ikkahran, koo-th'irukkahran
carriage	vaṇṭi	wunt'i

English.	Malayalam.	Pronunciation.
coach	kōccu-vaṇṭi	k*oh*chchŭ-wu*n*t'i
coachman	vaṇṭikkāran	wu*n*t'ik-k*ah*ran
cushion	metta	meththu
custom-house	cuṇka-p-pura, kasba	chōōṇgk'uppōōru, kusbu
custom-house officer	kasbā udyōgastan	kusb*ah* ōō*th*yo*h*gusthan
depart, to	puṟappeṭuka	pōōṟuppet'ōōk'u
departure	puṟappāṭȧ, yātṟa pōkkȧ	pooṟapp*ah*t'ŭ, y*ah*thṟu p*oh*kkŭ
engine	yantṟam, 'iñcan'	yen'thṟam, 'i*ny*ch'un'
expenses	cilavȧ	chiluwŭ
fare (charge)	vaṇṭikkūli	wu*n*t'ikkooli
guard	gāṟḍȧ	g*ah*ṟdŭ
guide	vaṟi-kāṭṭi	wuṟi-k*ah*tti
guide-book	vaṟi kāṭṭum pustakam	wuṟi k*ah*ttōōm pōōsth'uk'um
hat-box	toppi-p-peṭṭi	thoppi-p-petti
hotel	hōṭṭalȧ	h*oh*ttalŭ
interpreter	dvibāṣi, taṟjamakkāran	*th*wib*ah*shi. thuṟjamukk*ah*ran
key	tākkōlȧ	th*ah*kk*oh*lŭ
landlady	hōṭṭalkkāri	h*oh*ttalkk*ah*ri
landlord (hotel)	hōṭṭalkkāran	h*oh*ttalkk*ah*ran [ru
lavatory	kakkūs, maṟappura	kukkoos, muṟuppōō-
luggage	sāmānam	s*ah*m*ah*num
office	āppīsȧ	*ah*ppeesŭ
payment	kaṇakku-tīṟkkal	ku*n*ukkŭ-th'eeṟkkal
pier	jeṭṭi	jetti
porter	cumaṭṭu-kūli-kkāran	chōōmattŭ-k'ooli-kk*ah*ran [th'u
railway	tīvaṇṭi-p-pāta	thee-wu*n*t'i-p-p*ah*-
,, -carriage	tīvaṇṭi	theewu*n*t'i [sŭ
,, -station	tī-vaṇṭi-āppīsȧ	thee-wu*n*t'i-*ah*ppee-
receipt	ras'īti	raseeth'i
reins	vāṟȧ, lagān	w*ah*ṟŭ, lug*ah*n

English.	Malayalam.	Pronunciation.
road	vaṟi, nirattȧ, pāta	wuṟi, n'iraththŭ, p*ah*th'u
saddle	kutira-k-kōppȧ	kŏŏth'iru-k-k*oh*ppŭ
station master	tīvaṇṭi āppīssil mukya udyōgastan	theewu*n*t'i *ah*ppees-sil mŏŏkyu ŏŏ*thyoh* gusthan
steamer	āvikkappal	*ah*wi-k-kuppul
strap	tōl-vāṟȧ	th*oh*l-w*ah*ṟŭ
ticket	śīṭṭȧ	seettŭ
tourist	sañcāri	su*n*ych'*ah*ri
train (railway)	tī-vaṇṭi	thee-wu*n*t'i
voyage	kaṭal-yātṟa, kappal-yātṟa	kut'al-y*ah*thṟu, kuppul-y*ah*thṟu
waiter	viḷampan	wi*l*ump'an
waiting-room	kāttirikkum muṟi	k*ah*ththirikkŏŏm mŏŏṟi
whip	kuraṭāvȧ, cavukka	kŏŏrut'*ah*wŭ, chuwŏŏkku

Commercial and Trading Terms

(Kacca vaṭam sambandicca vākkukaḷ)

Account	kaṇakkȧ	ku*n*ukkŭ
,, , current	cellum kaṇakkȧ	chellŏŏm ku*n*ukkŭ
,, , joint	kūṭṭu-kaṇakkȧ	koottŭ-ku*n*ukkŭ
,, , to close an	eṭavāṭu nīṟttuka	et'uw*ah*t'u n'iṟththŏŏk'u
,, , to settle an	kaṇakku tīṟkkuka	ku*n*ukkŭ th'eeṟkkŏŏk'u
,, of sale	vilpana-k-kaṇakkȧ	wilpanu-k-ku*n*ukkŭ
acknowledgement	kaippaṟṟal arivippȧ	k*i*ppuṭṭul uriwippŭ
advance	muṅkūṟȧ	mŏŏngk'ooṟŭ
advice, letter	aṟiyikkum kattȧ	uṟiyikkŏŏm kuththŭ
agency	ējaṇṭāppīsȧ, ejaṇṭujōli	*ay*ja*n*t'*ah*ppeesŭ, *ay*ja*n*t'ŭj*oh*li
agent	ējaṇṭȧ	ayja*n*t'ŭ
apprentice	paṇi paṭikkunnavan	pu*n*i putikkŏŏn'n'uwun

English.	Malayalam.	Pronunciation.
arrangement	ēṟppāṭȧ	ayṟppaht'ŭ
arrears	kuṭis's'ika, bākki	kōōt'issik'u, bahkki
assets	mutalukaḷ	mōōth'alūkul
authorise, to	adikāra-p-peṭuttu-ka	uthikahruppet'ōōth-thōōk'u
average	śarāśari	surahsari
balance (remainder)	bākki, kaiyyiruppȧ	bahkki, kiyyirōōppŭ
balance sheet	bākki-t-taḷḷal paṭ-[ṭika	bahkki-th-thullal puttiku
bank	bāṅkȧ, huṇṭika	bahngk'ŭ, hōōnt'ik'u
bearer	koṇṭu varunna āḷ	kont'ŭwurōōn'n'u ahl
bill	billȧ, kaṇakku śīṭ-ṭȧ	billŭ, kunukkŭ seet-tŭ
„ of exchange	huṇṭiyal, paṇam māṟṟa billȧ	hōōnt'iyal, punum mahttu billŭ
bond, in	pāṇṭika śālayil	pahnt'ik'u sahlayil
bonded goods	pāṇṭika śālayil vec-ciṭṭuḷḷa sāmānaṇ-[ṇaḷ	pahnt'ik'u sahlayil wechchittōōllu sah-[mahnungngul
book-keeper	kaṇakku-piḷḷa	kunukkŭ-pillu
brokerage	tarakȧ	thurak'ŭ
business	pṟavṟtti, jōli, kār-yam, kaccavaṭam	pṟavrththi, johli, kahryam, kuchcha-wut'um
buyer	vāṅṅunnavan	wahngngōōn'n'uwun
cargo	kappal carakkȧ	kuppul churakkŭ
„ (freight)	ēṟṟukūli	ayttŭk'ooli
catalogue	sāmānappaṭṭika	sahmahnupputtik'u
cartage	vaṇṭikkūli	wunt'ikkooli
claim	avakāśam	uwukahsam
clearing house (customs)	cuṅkappura	chōōngk'uppōōru
clerk	gumastan	gōōmusth'un
commercial traveller	kaccavaṭa-k-karya-māy yātṟa ceyyun-navan	kuchchuwutu-k-kahryamahy yahthṟu cheyyōōn'n'uwun

English.	Malayalam.	Pronunciation.
company	kampani	kump'uni
„ , limited	kḷpta-k-kampani	kḷpthu-k-kump'ani
complaint	avalāti	uwul*ah*th'i
contract	karāṟȧ	kur*ah*ṟŭ
contractor	karāṟukāran	kur*ah*ṟŭk'*ah*run
cost, insurance freight (c.i.f.)	vila, inṣuvaṟkūli, ēṟṟukūli	wilu, inshoowuṟkoo-li, *ay*ṯṯŭkooli
credit balance	kaiyyiruppȧ	k*i*yyiroouppŭ
creditor	kaṭakkāran	kut'ukk*ah*run
customs duties	cuṅkam, tīruva	choongkum, thee-roowu
damages	cētam	ch*ay*th'um
damages, to claim	cētam cōdikkuka	ch*ay*thum ch*ohth*ik-kook'u
date, at three months	itȧ mutal mūnnu māsattil	ith'ŭ moothul moon-nŭ m*ah*suththil
debit and credit	cilavu-varavȧ	chiluwŭ-wuruwŭ
debtor	kaṭappuḷḷi	kut'uppoo*ll*i
deed	ādāram	*ahthah*ram
deliver, to	oppu koṭukka	oppŭ kot'ookku
delivered free	saujanyamāy oppu koṭutta	s*ow*janyum*ah*y oppŭ kot'ooththu
demurrage	paṭi	puṭ'i
director	ḍayaṟaktadōṟ	duyaṟukthu*thoh*ṟ
discount	kiṟivȧ	kiṟiwŭ
„ , to	iḷeccu koṭukka	i*l*echchŭ kot'ookku
dividend	lābavītam	l*ah*buweeth'um
dock and harbour dues	tuṟamuka-c-cuṅkam	thooṟumoookuch-choongk'um
duty, export	ēṟṟumati-c-cuṅkam	*ah*ṯṯoomuth'i-ch-choongk'um
„ -free	karam kotukkēṇṭ-ātta	kurum koṭookk*aynt*-*ah*ththu
„ , import	iṟakkumati-c-cuṅ-kam	iṟukkoomuthi-ch-choongkum
„ , liable to	cuṅkamuḷḷa	choongk'umoo*ll*u
enclosed	aṭakkam ceyta	ut'ukkum cheyth'u

English.	Malayalam.	Pronunciation.
enclosure	aṭakkam	ut'ukkum
endorse, to	inḍōssu ceyka	indohssŭ cheyk'u
exchange (of money	paṇam māṟṟam	punum mahṯṯum
factory	yantṟaśāla	yan'thṟusahlu
the firm	kaccavaṭakkāṟ	kuchchuwut'ukkahṟ
forwarding	ayakkal	uyakkul
,, agent	ayakkum ējaṇṭȧ	uyakkōōm ayjant'ŭ
gross weight	motta-t-tūkkam	moththuth--thook-kum
guarantee	uttaravādam	ōōththuruwahthum
I.O.U.	pṟōnōṭṭȧ	prohnohttŭ
import and export	iṟakkumatiyum ēṟ-ṟumatiyum	iṟukkōōmuth'iyōōm ayṯṯōōmuth'iyōōm[
income	varavȧ	wuruwŭ
information	vaṟtamānam	wuṟthumahnam
insurance	inṣuvaṟ ceyyal	inshōōwuṟ cheyyal
,, broker	inṣuvaṟ ceyyum dallāḷi	inshōōwuṟ cheyyōōm thullahli
,, company	nȧṣṭapālana-k-kampani	n'usht'upahlunu-k-kumpani
,, policy	inṣuvaṟ ceyyum ā-dāram	inshōōwuṟ cheyyōōm ahthahram
,, premium	inṣuvaṟ ceyvānuḷḷa nirakkȧ	inshōōwuṟ cheywah-nōōllu n'irakkŭ
interest	paliśa	pulisu
lease	pāttam, kāṇam	pahttum, kahnum
,, -holder	pāttadār, kānam-dār	pahttuthahṟ,kahnum-thahṟ
liabilities	kaṭam, kaṭama	kut'um, kut'umu
load, to	cumaṭȧ kēṟṟuka	chōōmat'ŭ kayṯṯōō-k'u
loss	naṣṭam, cētam	nusht'am, chayth'am
manager	kāryakkāran	kahryakkahran
market	canta	chun'th'u
,, , foreign	paradēśa-c-canta	puruthaysu-ch-chun'th'u
,, , home	nāṭṭu-canta	nahttŭ-chun'th'u

English.	Malayalam.	Pronunciation.
market day	canta divasam	chun'th'u *th*iwasum
,, dues	canta vāṭaka	chun'th'u w*ah*t'ak'u
,, price	canta vila, nirakkȧ	chun'th'u wilu, n'i-rakkŭ
negotiable, saleable	eṭavāṭu ceyyāvun-na, vilkkāvunna	et'uw*ah*t'ŭ cheyy*ah*-wo͞on'n'u,wilkk*ah*-wo͞on'n'u
order (for goods)	āvaśyappeṭal	*ah*wasyuppet'ul
packing	keṭṭal	kettal
partnership	kūṭṭukaccavaṭam	koottŭk'uchchawu-t'um
payable	koṭukkēṇṭiya	koto͞okk*ayn*t'iyu
(6) per cent	nūṟṟinȧ (āṟu) vītam	n'ooṯṯinŭ (*ah*ṟŭ) weeth'am
per centage	śatamānam	suth'um*ah*num
price	vila	wilu
,, , list	vila-vivara-ppaṭṭi-ka	wilu-wiwuru-p-put-tiku
,, , selling-	vilkkunna vila	wilko͞on'n'u wilu
,, , wholesale	motta vila	moththu wilu
property	vastu, āsti	wusth'o͞o, *ah*sth'i
quotation (of price)	vila paṟayal	wilu puṟayul
ready money	ṟokkam	ṟokkum
earnest money	accāram	uchch*ah*rum
receipt	raśīti, rasītȧ	ruseeth'i, raseeth'ŭ
registered letter	ṟajistṟȧ kattȧ	rajisthṟŭ kuththŭ
,, tonnage	rajistṟākkappeṭṭa kappalttūkkam	rajisthṟ*ah*kkuppettu kuppulththookkum
registration fee	rajistṟȧ kūli	rajisthṟŭ kooli
rent	vāṭaka	w*ah*t'uku
representative	pṟatinidi	pṟath'in'i*th*i
retail	cillaṟa	chilluṟu
,, , to sell by	cillaṟayāy vilkkuka	chilluṟuy*ah*y wilk ko͞ok'u
salesman (seller)	vilkkunnavan	wilko͞on'n'uwan
settling day	eṭavāṭu tīṟkkum divasam	et'uw*ah*t'ŭ theeṟk ko͞om *th*iwasum

English.	Malayalam.	Pronunciation.
share	ōhari, paṅkȧ,	*oh*huri, puṉgk'ŭ
ship, to	kappalil ēṟṟuka	kuppalil *ay*ṯṯo͞ok'u
shipping charges	kappal-k-kūli	kuppal-k-kooli
„ firm	kappalil carakku kēṟṟunna kampani	kuppalil churukkŭ k*ay*ṯṯo͞on'n'u kump'ani
solvent	kaṭam tīrppān mutaluḷḷa	kut'um theeṟpp*ah*n mo͞oth'alo͞o*ll*u
stock	kaivaśam uḷḷa carakkȧ	k*i*wusum o͞o*ll*u churakkŭ
stock-broker	dallāḷi	*th*ull*ah*l*i*
trade (in general)	kaccavaṭam	kuchchuwut'um
wharf	sāmāna jeṭṭi	s*ah*m*ah*nu jetti
wharfage	jeṭṭi vāṭaka	jetti w*ah*t'ak'u
wholesale	mottamāy	moththum*ah*y

Post Office and Telegrams

(Tappālāppīsum Kampikaḷum)

English	Malayalam	Pronunciation
Book post	pustaka-t-tappāl	po͞osth'uk'u-th-thup [p*ah*l
cable (telegraph)	kampi	kump'i
cable, to	kampi aṭikkuka	kump'i ut'ikko͞ok'u
letter post	eṟuttȧ tappāl	eṟo͞oththŭ thupp*ah*l
money order	maṇi āṭaṟ, tappāl huṇṭi	mu*n*i *ah*t'uṟ, thupp*ah*l ho͞o*n*t'i
parcel post	baṅki-t-tappāl	buṉgk'i-th-thupp*ah*l
postage paid	tappāl-k-kūli aṭacca	thupp*ah*l-k-kooli ut'achchu
postage stamp	tappāl mudra	thupp*ah*l mo͞o*th*ru
post-(pillar) box	kattu peṭṭi	kuththŭ petti
postman	tappāl śipāyi	thupp*ah*l sip*ah*yi
postmaster	tappāl mēṣṭṟȧ	thupp*ah*l m*ay*shtṟŭ
post office	tappāl āppīsȧ	thupp*ah*l *ah*ppeesŭ
register, to	ṟajistṟākkuka	ṟajisthṟ*ah*kko͞ok'u

English.	Malayalam.	Pronunciation.
reply paid	maṟuvaṭikku kūli muṅkūṟaṭacca	muṟoowut'ikkū kooli moongk'ooṟut'ach-chu
telegraph form	kampi-k-kaṭalassá	kumpi-k-kut'ulahs-sū
„ messenger	kampi-ś-śipāyi	kump'i-s-sıpahyi
telephone	kampi vaṟi samsā-rippānuḷḷa yantṟam	kump'i-wuṟi sumsah-rippahnoollu yan'-thṟum
to be called for	vanná.avaśyappe-ṭēṇṭiya	wun'n'ū ahvasyup-petaynt'iyu

Shooting and Fishing

(Nāyāṭṭum matsyam piṭikkalum)

Axe (hatchet)	kōtāli	koht'ahli
bait, to bait	ira ; ira iṭuka	iru ; iru it'ook'u
bank (of a river)	kara, tīram	kuru ; theeram
basket	kuṭṭa	koottu
bite, a	kaṭi	kut'i
boat	vañci, tōṇi	wunych'i, thohni
boat-hook	vañci-k-kokki	wunych'i-k-kokki
boatman	vañcikkāran	wunychikkahran
boatman's pole	kaṟukkōlá	kuṟookkohlū
breech (of a gun)	veṭi-t-tuḷa	wet'i-th-thoolu
bullet	uṇṭa, veṭi-y-uṇṭa	oont'u, wet'i-y-oon-t'u
caps	vaṟtti	wuṟththi
cartridge extractor	tōṭṭa nīkki	thohttu n'eekki
cartridges	tōṭṭa	thohttu
cord (string)	caraṭa	churat'ū
double-barrelled	iraṭṭa-k-kuṟal	iruttukkooṟal
file	aram	uram
fish	matsyam, mīn	mulsyam, meen
„ , to	matsyam piṭikkuka	mulsyam pit'ikkoo-k'u

English.	Malayalam.	Pronunciation.
fisherman	matsyam piṭuttakkāran	mulsyam pit'o͝oth-thukk*ah*ran
" (caste)	mukkuvan	mo͝okko͝owun
fishing, angling	matsyam piṭuttam, [cūṇṭaliṭal	mulsyam piṭo͝oth-thum, choo*n*t'alit'al
" basket	matsya-k-kuṭṭa	mulsyu-k-ko͝ottu
" hook	cūṇṭal koḷuttȧ	choo*n*t'al ko*l*o͝oththŭ
" line	cūṇṭal-c-caraṭȧ	choo*n*t'al-ch-churatŭ
" rod	cūṇṭal-vaṭi	choo*n*t'al-wut'i
" tackle	cūṇṭal-sāmānaṅṅaḷ	choo*n*t'al-s*ah*m*ah*-nuṉgṉgu*l*
float	mitappȧ	mith'uppŭ
fly	puṟu	po͝oṟo͝o
game bag	vēṭṭa-s-sañci	w*a*yttu-s-su*ny*ch'i
gun	tōkkȧ	th*oh*kkŭ
gun-case	tōkku-peṭṭi	th*oh*kkŭ-petti
gun-powder	veṭi-marunnȧ	wet'i-muro͝on'n'ŭ
hammer (of gun)	(tōkkin) kutira	th*oh*kkin ko͝oth'iru
knife	katti	kuththi
match-box	tī-p-peṭṭi	thee-p-petti
matches	ti-p-peṭṭi-k-kōlȧ	thee-p-petti-k-k*oh*lŭ
nail	āṇi	*ahn*i
net, casting	vīśu-vala	weesŭ-wulu
" , draw	kara-vala	kuru-wulu
" , fishing	vala	wulu
" , large sea-	cīna-vala	cheenu-wulu
pistol	pistōḷ	pisth'*ohl*
revolver	kaittōkkȧ	k*i*thth*oh*kkŭ
saw, hand-	kaivāḷȧ	k*i*w*ahl*ŭ
screw	piriyāṇi, iskūṟāṇi	piriy*ahn*i, iskoo-ṟ*ahn*i
screwdriver	iskūrȧ muṟukki	iskoorŭ mo͝oṟo͝okki
spanner	kaṭṭa muṟukki	kuttu mo͝oṟo͝okki
sheath	uṟa	o͝oṟu
shot	ṟava	ṟuwu
sport (hunting)	nāyāṭṭȧ, vēṭṭa	n'*ah*y*ah*ttŭ, w*a*yttu

English.	Malayalam.	Pronunciation.
sportsman	nāyāṭṭukāran, ṣikkāri	n'*ah*yahttŭk'*ah*ran, shikk*ah*ri
tools	āyudaṅṅaḷ, karukkaḷ, uḷikaḷ	*ah*yōō*th*uṉgṉgu*l*, kurōōkku*l*, ōō*l*iku*l*

Cardinal Numbers

One	onnȧ	on'n'ŭ
two	raṇṭȧ	ru*n*t'ŭ
three	mūnnȧ	moon'n'ŭ
four	nālȧ	n'*ah*lŭ
five	añcȧ	u*ny*ch'ŭ
six	āṟȧ	*ah*ṟŭ
seven	ēṟȧ	*ay*ṟŭ
eight	eṭṭȧ	ettŭ
nine	ompatȧ	omp'uth'ŭ
ten	pattȧ	puththŭ
eleven	patin-onnȧ	puth'in-on'n'ŭ
twelve	pan-t-ṟaṇṭȧ	pun'th--ṟu*n*t'ŭ
thirteen	pati-mūnnȧ	puth'i-moon'n'ŭ
fourteen	patin-nālȧ	puth'in'-n'*ah*lŭ
fifteen	patin-añcȧ	puth'in-u*ny*ch'a
sixteen	patin-āṟȧ	puth'in-*ah*ṟŭ
seventeen	patin-ēṟȧ	puth'in-*ay*ṟŭ
eighteen	patin-eṭṭȧ	puth'in-ettŭ
nineteen	pat-t-ompatȧ	puth-th-omp'uth'ŭ
twenty	irupatȧ	irōōp'uth'ŭ
twenty-one	irupat-t-onnȧ	irōōp'uth-th-on'n'ŭ
twenty-two	irupatti-raṇṭȧ	irōōp'uththi-ru*n*t'ŭ
twenty-three	irupatti-mūnnȧ	irōōp'uththi-moon'-n'ŭ
thirty	muppatȧ	mōōpputh'ŭ
forty	nālpatȧ	n*ah*lputhŭ
fifty	aympatȧ	uymp'uth'ŭ
sixty	aṟupatȧ	uṟōōp'uth'ŭ
seventy	eḻupatȧ	eṟōōp'uth'ŭ
eighty	eṇpatȧ	e*n*p'uth'ŭ

English.	Malayalam.	Pronunciation.
ninety	toṇ-ṇūṟȧ	th*on*-*noo*ṟŭ
100	nūṟȧ	n'ooṟŭ
101	nūṟ-ṟ-onnȧ	n'ooṭ-ṭ-on'n'ŭ
103	nūṟṟi-mūnnȧ	n'ooṭṭi-moon'n'ŭ
200	iru-n-nūṟȧ	iro͝o-n'-n'ooṟŭ
300	mun-nūṟȧ	mon'-n'ooṟŭ
400	nā-nūṟȧ	n'*ah*-nooṟŭ
500	añ-ñūṟȧ	u*ny*-*ny*ooṟŭ
600	aṟun-nūṟȧ	uṟo͝on'-n'ooṟŭ
700	eṟu-n-nūṟȧ	eṟo͝on'-n'ooṟŭ
800	eṇ-ṇūṟȧ	e*n*-*noo*ṟŭ
900	toḷḷāyiram	tho*llah*yiram
1000	āyiram	*ah*yiram
1001	āyiratti-onnȧ	*ah*yiraththi-on'n'ŭ
1100	āyiratti-oru-nūṟȧ	*ah*yiraththi-oro͝o-n'ooṟŭ
2000	raṇṭāyiram	ru*nt'ah*yiram
10000	patin-āyiram	puthin-*ah*yiram
100000	lakṣam	lak'shum
1925	āyiratti-t-toḷḷāyirat-ti-irupat-t-añcȧ	*ah*yiraththi-th-tho*l*-*lah*yiraththi-iro͝o-puth-th-u*ny*ch'ŭ

Ordinal Numbers

English.	Malayalam.	Pronunciation.
First	ādyatte, onnāmatte	*ahth*yaththe, on'n'-*ah*muththe
second	raṇṭāmatte	ru*nt'ah*muththe
third	mūnnāmatte	moon'n'*ah*muththe
fourth	nālāmatte	n'*ah*l*ah*muththe
fifth	añcāmatte	u*ny*ch'*ah*muththe
sixth	āṟāmatte	*ah*ṟ*ah*muththe
seventh	ēṟāmatte	*ay*ṟ*ah*muththe
eighth	eṭṭāmatte	ett*ah*muththe
ninth	ompatāmatte	omp'uth'*ah*muththe
tenth	puttāmatte	puthth*ah*muththe
eleventh	patin-onnāmatte	puthin-on'n'*ah*-muththe

English.	Malayalam.	Pronunciation.
twelfth	pan-t-ṟaṇṭāmatte	pun'-th-ṟu*n*t'*ah*-muththe
thirteenth	patimūnnāmatte	puth'imoon'n'*ah*-muththe
fourteenth	patinnālāmatte	puth'in'n'*ah*l*ah*-muththe
fifteenth	patinañcāmatte	puth'inu*ny*ch'*ah*-muththe
sixteenth	patināṟāmatte	puth'in*ah*ṟ*ah*muth-the
seventeenth	patinēṛāmatte	puth'in*ay*ṛ*ah*muth-the
eighteenth	patineṭṭāmatte	puth'inett*ah*muththe
nineteenth	pattompatāmatte	puththomp'uth'*ah*-muththe
twentieth	irupatāmatte	iro͝op'uth'*ah*muththe
twentyfirst	irupatt'onnāmatte	iro͝op'uthth'on'n'*ah*-muththe
twenty-second	irupatti-raṇṭāmatte	iro͝op'uththi-ru*n*t'*ah*-muththe
thirtieth	muppatāmatte	mo͝opputh'*ah*muth-the
fortieth	nālpatāmatte	n'*ah*lputh'*ah*muth-the
fiftieth	aympatāmatte	uymp'uth'*ah*muth-the
sixtieth	aṟupatāmatte	uṟo͝op'uth'*ah*muth-the
seventieth	eṛupatāmatte	eṛo͝op'uth'*ah*muth-the
eightieth	eṇpatāmatte	e*n*p'uth'*ah*muththe
ninetieth	toṇṇūṟāmatte	tho*nn*ooṟ*ah*muththe
hundredth	nūṟāmatte	n'ooṟ*ah*muththe
101st	nūṟṟ'onnāmatte	n'ooṯṯ'on'n'*ah*muth-the
102nd	nūṟṟi-raṇṭāmatte	n'ooṯṯi-ru*n*t'*ah*muth-the
200th	irun-nūṟāmatte	iro͝on'-n'ooṟ*ah*muth-the

English.	Malayalam.	Pronunciation.
300th	munnūṟāmatte	mo͝on'-n'ooṟ*ah*muth-the
1000th	āyirāmatte	*ah*yir*ah*muththe
1001st	āyiratti-onnāmatte	*ah*yiraththi-on'n'*ah*-muththe
last	oṭuvilatte, avasānatte	ot'o͝owilaththe, uwu-s*ah*nuththe
firstly	ādyam, ādyamāy	*ahth*yam, *ahth*ya-m*ahy*
secondly	raṇṭāmatȧ, raṇṭāmatāy	ru*nt*'*ah*muth'ŭ, ru*n*-t'*ah*muth'*ahy*
fifthly	añcāmatȧ, añcāmatāy	u*ny*ch*ah*muth'ŭ, u*ny*-ch*ah*muth'*ahy*
lastly	oṭuvil, avasānamāy	ot'o͝owil, uwus*ah*na-m*ahy*

Collective Numbers, &c.

A couple, pair	jōṭȧ, iṇa, peṭṭa	jo*h*t'ŭ, i*n*u, pettu
double, twice (adj.)	iraṭṭa	iruttu
dozen	pantṟaṇṭȧ, ḍajan	pun'thṟu*nt*'ŭ, dujan
one fifth	añcil onnȧ	u*ny*chil on'n'ŭ
one sixteenth	mākāṇi	m*ah*k*ah*ni
three sixteenths	muṇṭāṇi	mo͝o*nt*'*ah*ni
one eighth	arakkāl	urakk*ah*l
one fourth	kāl	k*ah*l
half	ara	uru
once	orikkal, oru prāvas'yam	orikkul, oro͝o pṟ*ah*-wasyum yum
thrice	mūnnu prāvaśyam	moon'n'ŭ pṟ*ah*was-
score	irupatȧ	iro͝op'uth'ŭ
single	oṟṟa	oṯṯu
one third	mūnnil-onnȧ	moon'n'il-on'n'ŭ
three quarters	mukkāl	mo͝okk*ah*l
seven-eighths	mukkāle-arakkāl	mo͝okk*ah*le-urakk*ah*l
fifteen-sixteenths	mukkāle-muṇṭāṇi	mo͝okk*ah*le-mo͝o*n*-t'*ah*ni
two and a half	raṇṭara	ru*nt*'uru

THE NUMERALS.

Cardinals.

	Malay-alam Signs.	Name	Adjectival Form.
1	൧	ഒന്നു° onnȧ	ഒരു oru before consonants*; ഓർ or before vowels†
2	൨	രണ്ടു° raṇṭȧ	ഇരു iru, ഈർ ir, രണ്ടു° raṇṭȧ (ഇരുവർ iruvar, *two persons.*
3	൩	മൂന്നു° mūnnȧ	മു mu, മൂന്ന munnȧ (മുക്കണ്ണൻ mukkaṇ-ṇan, *the three-eyed.*)
4	൪	നാലു° nālȧ	നാൽ nāl, നാലു° nālȧ (നാല്ക്കാലി nālk-kāli, *a stool, a quadruped.*)
5	൫	അഞ്ചു° añcȧ	ഐ ai, അഞ്ചു° añcȧ (ഐയ്യമ്പൻ aiyyampan, *the god with five arrows. Eros.*
6	൬	ആറു° āṟȧ	അറു aṟu, ആറ് āṟȧ (അറുപതു° aṟupatȧ, *sixty.*
7	൭	ഏഴു° ēṟȧ	എഴു eṟu, ഏഴ് ēṟȧ.
8	൮	എട്ടു° eṭṭȧ	എൺ eṇ എട്ട് eṭṭȧ

*As ഒരു ചെറുക്കൻ oru ceṟukkan, *a boy.*

†As ഒരപ്പം orappam, *a loaf.* See (footnote on section on Articles)

	Malayalam Signs.	Name.
9	൯	ഒമ്പതു് ompatá
10	൧൦	പത്തു് pattá.
11	൧൧	പതിനൊന്നു് patinonná
12	൧൨	പന്ത്രണ്ടു് pantṛaṇṭá.
13	൧൩	പതിമൂന്നു് patimūnná
14	൧൪	പതിന്നാലു് patinnālá.
15	൧൫	പതിനഞ്ചു് patinañcá.
16	൧൬	പതിനാറു് patināṛá.
17	൧൭	പതിനേഴു് patinēṛá.
18	൧൮	പതിനെട്ടു് patineṭṭá.
19	൧൯	പത്തൊമ്പതു് pattompatá.
20	൨൦	ഇരുപതു് irupatá. ഇരുവതു് iruvatá
21	൨൧	ഇരുപത്തൊന്നു് irupattonná.
22	൨൨	ഇരുപത്തിരണ്ടു് irupattiraṇṭá.
23	൨൩	ഇരുപത്തിമൂന്നു് irupattimūnná.
30	൩൦	മുപ്പതു് muppatá.
40	൪൦	നാല്പതു് nālpatá
50	൫൦	ഐമ്പതു്, അയ്മ്പതു് aimpatá, aympatá.
60	൬൦	അറുപതു് aṛupatá.
70	൭൦	എഴുപതു് eṛupatá.
80	൮൦	എൺപതു് eṇpatá.
90	൯൦	തൊണ്ണൂറു് toṇṇūṛá.

	Malayalam Signs.	Name.
100	൧൦൦	നൂറ് nūṟȧ.
101	൧൦൧	നൂറ്റൊന്ന് nūṟṟonnȧ.
200	൨൦൦	ഇരുനൂറ് irunnūṟȧ.
300	൩൦൦	മുന്നൂറ് munnūṟȧ.
400	൪൦൦	നാനൂറ് nānūṟȧ.
500	൫൦൦	അഞ്ഞൂറ് aññūṟȧ.
600	൬൦൦	അറുനൂറ് arunnūṟȧ.
700	൭൦൦	ഏഴുനൂറ് eṛunnūṟȧ.
800	൮൦൦	എണ്ണൂറ് eṇṇūṟȧ.
900	൯൦൦	തൊള്ളായിരം toḷḷāyiram.
1,000	൧൦൦൦	ആയിരം āyiram.
1,001	൧൦൦൧	ആയിരത്തൊന്ന് āyirattonnȧ.
1,002	൧൦൦൨	ആയിരത്തിരണ്ട് ȧyirattiraṇṭȧ.
1,100	൧൧൦൦	ആയിരത്തൊരുനൂറ് āyirattoṛunūṟȧ.
1,200	൧൨൦൦	അയിരത്തിരുനൂറ് āyirattirunnūṟȧ.
1,900	൧൯൦൦	ആയരിത്തിത്തൊള്ളായിരം āyarittittoḷḷāyiram.
1,926	൧൯൨൬	ആയിരത്തിത്തൊള്ളായിരത്തിരുപത്തിയാറ് āyirattit-toḷḷāyirat-tirupatti-yāṟȧ.
2,000	൨൦൦൦	രണ്ടായിരം raṇṭāyiram.
3,000	൩൦൦൦	മൂവ്വായിരം muvvāyiram, etc.
100,000	൧൦൦൦൦൦	ലക്ഷം lakṣam.

THE PARTS OF SPEECH.

ARTICLES.

In Malayāḷam there is no article to represent the English *a* (*an*) or *the*. Thus, മകൾ (makaḷ) may mean *a daughter* or *the daughter*, just as Tamil makaḷ or Sanskrit putrī. But ഒരു (oru) and ഓർ (or), the adjectival forms of ഒന്ന് (onnă) *one* are sometimes used as substitutes for *a* or *an*, the former before a consonant and the latter before a vowel, as ഒരു മകൾ (oru makaḷ) *a daughter* and ഓരാണി (orāṇi)* *a nail*. Besides the demonstrative prefixes അ, and ഇ (see section *b* page 70), and a few postpositions of emphasis, such as ആയവൻ (āyavan), ആയവൾ (āyavaḷ), ആയത് (āyată), എന്നവൻ (e'nnavan), etc., Malayāḷam has no equivalent for the English definite article *the*.

NOUNS.

Gender and Number.

(i). All Malayāḷam nouns are divided into two main classes, namely, സചേതനങ്ങൾ sacētanaṅṅaḷ, *rational*, and അചേതനങ്ങൾ acētanaṅṅaḷ, *irrational*.

The former comprises all rational beings, as gods, men, etc., and has, therefore, two genders, masculine and feminine; while the latter, which includes all irrational beings and inanimate objects, as cats, dogs, trees, truth, goodness, etc., has only the neuter gender. Hence, words such as മൂരി mūri, *a bull*, പിടിയാന piṭiyāna, *a she-elephant*, though really masculine and feminine respectively, are yet treated as neuter nouns, the pronouns used in referring to them being always put in the neuter; as, മൂരി എവിടെ? ഞങ്ങൾ അതിനെ വിറ്റു കളഞ്ഞു mūri eviṭe? ñaṅṅaḷ atine viṭṭu kaḷaññu, *Where is the bull? we have sold it*. (not avane, masc.).

---

* orāṇi = or + āni.

(ii). The gender is also indicated by means of the terminations: ṅ (an, ān, attān) for the masculine singular nominative: i, aḷ, (tti, atti, ātti. cci, ṭṭi) for the feminine: am, tȧ, or atȧ for the neuter; e.g.

Masc.	Fem.	Neut.
കള്ളൻ *a thief*	കള്ളി *a she-thief*	കള്ളം *a lie*
kaḷḷan	kaḷḷi	kaḷḷam
അവൻ *he*	അവൾ *she*	അത *it*
avan	avaḷ	atȧ
മാരാൻ *a drummer*	മാരാത്തി *a she-drummer*	
mārān	mārātti	
കൊല്ലൻ *a blacksmith*	കൊല്ലത്തി *a she-blacksmith*	
kollan	kollatti	
തടിയൻ *a fat man*	തടിച്ചി *a fat woman*	തടിച്ചത *a fat thing*
taṭiyan	taticci	taṭiccatȧ
തമ്പുരാൻ *a lord*	തമ്പുരാട്ടി *a lady* (title)	
tampurān	tampurāṭṭi	

The genders of nouns that do not have these endings can be known by their meaning; e.g.

Masc.	Fem.	Neut.
അച്ഛൻ *father*	അമ്മ *mother*	മാങ്ങ *a mango*
accan	amma	māṅṅa
ഭർത്താവ് *husband*	ഭാര്യ *wife*	കാട് *a forest*
bartāva	bārya	kāṭȧ
മൂരി *a bull*	പശു, പയ്യ് *a cow*	കുട *an umbrella*
mūri	paśu, pay'ya	kuṭa

(iii). The plural of nouns is formed by the addition of കൾ kaḷ ക്കൾ (kkaḷ) to the crude form; but masculine nouns ending in n (an, ān, etc.; see (ii) above) invariably, and other nouns by way of respect, take മാർ mār, and not kaḷ. Thus:—

Sing.	Plur.
ചതിയൻ *a treacherous man*	ചതിയന്മാർ *treacherous men*
catiyan	catiyanmār
കുട്ടി *a child*	കുട്ടികൾ *children*
kuṭṭi	kuṭṭikaḷ
അമ്മ *mother*	അമ്മമാർ *mothers*
amma	ammamār
പശു *a cow*	പശുക്കൾ *cows*
paśu	paśukkaḷ
പടം *a picture*	പടങ്ങൾ *pictures*
paṭam	paṭaṅṅaḷ

The termination അർ ar is, however, added to nouns ending in n to indicate the common gender in the Plural, or respect in the singular. The super-addition of kaḷ to these, and of mār to Plurals ending in kaḷ give the Plural number indicated with respect. Thus:—

Sing.	Plur.
avan, *he*	avar, *they* avarkaḷ, *Esq.*
manuṣyan, *a man*	manuṣyanmār, *men* manuṣyar, *mankind*
kuṭiyan, *a drunkard* (masc.)	kuṭiyanmār, *drunkards* (masc.) kuṭiyar, *drunkards* (com. gen.)
guru, *a teacher*	(gurukkaḷ-mār) = gurukkanmar, *teachers*

Neuter nouns in ത് tă either add kaḷ, or change tă into വ va in the plural, e.g. നല്ലത് nallata, *a good thing*, നല്ലതുകൾ nallatukaḷ, or നല്ലവ nallava, *good things*.

Declension.

In the following model, the case endings are separated from the stem by hyphens for the sake of clearness. These endings are the same for all nouns, singular and plural.

(a) 1. Nominative — ചെറുക്കൻ *a boy.*
cerukkan

2. Accusative — ചെറുക്കനെ *a boy*
cerukkan-e

3. Instrumental or Ablative of connection — ചെറുക്കനാൽ *by a boy.*
cerukkan-āl
ചെറുക്കനോടു (together) *with a boy.*
cerukkan-ōṭá

4. Dative — (ചെറുക്കൻ—ക്കു =)
(cerukkan-kká =)
ചെറുക്കനു, ചെറുക്കന്നു *to a boy, for a boy.*
cerukkaná, cerukkanná*

5. Ablative of place, whence — ചെറുക്കനിൽനിന്ന് *from a boy.*
cerukkan-ilninná†

6. Genitive — (ചെറുക്കൻ—ഉടെ =)
(cerukkan-uṭe)
ചെറുക്കന്റെ *of a boy.*
cerukkan-ṟe*

7. Locative — ചെറുക്കനിൽ *at, in,* or *with a boy.*
cerukkan-il
ചെറുക്കങ്കൽ
cerukkaṅ-kal

8. Vocative — ചെറുക്കാ *O boy.*
cerukk-ā

---

* After a noun ending in n, the dative termination kká is reduced by assimilation with n to nná, or simply ná. The genitive uṭe is similarly reduced to nṟe. The same applies to nouns declined with the euphonic increment "in" (See page 68).

† ilninna is a combination of ഇൽ-നിന്ന il-ninná, *standing from* ·ninná is the gerund of nil. See below, para. ii, page 119

(*b*) The plural of cerukkan is, as explained above, ചെറുക്കന്മാർ cerukkanmār. To this, case terminations are added as in the singular; e.g. Acc. ചെറുക്കന്മാരെ cerukkanmāre, Dative ചെറുക്കന്മാൎക്കു cerukkanmārkka, Gen. ചെറുക്കന്മാരുടെ cerukkanmāruṭe, etc.

(*c*) Exceptions :—

(1) Nouns ending in m, change m into tt in the singular before adding case suffixes; as കുടം kuṭam, *a pot*, Acc. കുടത്തെ kuṭatte, *a pot*, Gen. കുടത്തിന്റെ kuṭattinṟe, *of a pot*.

(2) The increment ഇൻ in is often to be inserted between the noun and the case endings; കല്ലിന്റെ kallinṟe (= kal-in-uṭe), *of a stone;* ധനത്തിനു danattinå, (=danam-in-kkå) *for wealth.*

PRONOUNS.

Pronouns are declined in the same way as nouns, and with the same case endings. In the oblique cases, however, some of them change the root, as may be seen from the following models :—

(*a*) Personal Pronouns.

(i.) FIRST PERSON.

Singular.

1. Nom.	ഞാൻ ñān	*I*
2. Acc.	എന്നെ enne	*me*
3. Instr.	എന്നാൽ ennāl	*by me.*
	എന്നോടു ennōṭa	*with me.*
4. Dat.	എനിക്കു enikkå	*to me, for me.*
5. Abl.	എന്നിൽനിന്നു ennilninnå	*from me.*
6. Gen.	എന്റെ enṟe	*of me.*
7. Loc.	എന്നിൽ ennil	*in me.*
	എങ്കൽ eṅkal	*with me.*

Plural.

1. Nom.	നമ്മൾ, ഞങ്ങൾ* nammaḷ, ñaṅṅaḷ	*we.*
2. Acc.	നമ്മളെ, ഞങ്ങളെ nammaḷe, ñaṅṅaḷe	*us.*
3. Instr.	നമ്മളാൽ, ഞങ്ങളാൽ nammaḷāl, ñaṅṅaḷāl	*by us.*
	നമ്മളോട്, ഞങ്ങളോട nammaḷōṭȧ, ñaṅṅaḷōṭȧ	*with us.*
4. Dat.	നമ്മൾക്ക്, ഞങ്ങൾക്ക് nammaḷkkȧ, ñaṅṅaḷkkȧ	*to us, for us.*
5. Abl.	നമ്മളിൽനിന്ന്, ഞങ്ങളിൽനിന്ന് nammaḷilninnȧ, ñaṅṅaḷilninnȧ	*from us.*
6. Gen.	നമ്മളുടെ, ഞങ്ങളുടെ nammaḷuṭe, ñaṅṅaḷuṭe	*our.*
7. Loc.	നമ്മളിൽ, ഞങ്ങളിൽ nammaḷil, ñaṅṅaḷil	*in us.*
	നമ്മളിങ്കൽ, ഞങ്ങളിങ്കൽ nammaḷiṅkal, ñaṅṅaḷiṅkal	*with us.*

(ii.) SECOND PERSON.

Singular.

1. Nom.	നീ nī	*thou.*
2. Acc.	നിന്നെ ninne	*thee.*
3. Instr.	നിന്നാൽ, നിന്നോട ninnāl, ninnōṭȧ	*by* or *with thee.*
4. Dat.	നിനക്ക് ninakkȧ	*to* or *for thee.*
5. Abl.	നിന്നിൽനിന്ന് ninnilninnȧ	*from thee.*
6. Gen.	നിന്റെ ninṟe	*thy.*
7. Loc.	നിന്നിൽ, നിങ്കൽ ninnil, niṅkal	*in* or *with thee.*

* നമ്മൾ nammaḷ includes the person spoken to, ഞങ്ങൾ ñaṅṅaḷ excludes.

Plural.

1. Nom.	നിങ്ങൾ niṅṅaḷ	*you.*
2. Acc.	നിങ്ങളെ niṅṅaḷe	*you.*
3. Instr.	നിങ്ങളാൽ, നിങ്ങളോട niṅṅaḷāl, niṅṅaḷōṭȧ	*by* or *with you.*
4. Dat.	നിങ്ങൾക്ക niṅṅaḷkkȧ	*to* or *for you.*
5. Abl.	നിങ്ങളിൽനിന്ന് niṅṅaḷilninnȧ	*from you.*
6. Gen.	നിങ്ങളുടെ niṅṅaḷuṭe	*your.*
7. Loc.	നിങ്ങളിൽ, നിങ്ങളിങ്കൽ niṅṅaḷil, niṅṅaḷiṅkal	*in* or *with you.*

(*b*) Demonstrative Pronouns.

(or Personal Pronouns of the Third Person.)

Singular.

	Masc.	Fem.	Neut.
1. Nom.	അവൻ *he* avan	അവൾ *she* avaḷ	അത് *it.* atȧ
2. Acc.	അവനെ *him* avane	അവളെ *her* avaḷe	അതിനെ *it.* atine
3. Instr.	അവനാൽ *by him* avanāl	അവളാൽ *by her* avaḷāl	അതിനാൽ *by it.* atināl
	അവനോട *with him* avanōṭȧ	അവളോട് *with her* avaḷōṭạ	അതിനോട് *with it.* atinōṭȧ
4. Dat.	അവന്ന്, അവന് *to* or *for him* avannȧ avanȧ,	അവൾക്ക് *to* or *for her* avaḷkkȧ	അതിന്ന്, അതിന *to* or *for it.* atinnȧ atinȧ

5. Abl. അവനിൽനിന്ന *from him* അവളിൽനിന്ന് *from her*
avanilninnå avaḷilninnå
അതിൽനിന്ന് *from it.*
atilninna

6. Gen. അവന്റെ *his* അവളുടെ *her* അതിന്റെ *its..*
avanṟe avaḷuṭe atinṟe

7. Loc. അവനിൽ *in him* അവളിൽ *in her* അതിൽ *in it*
avanil avaḷil atil
അവങ്കൽ *with him* അവളിങ്കൽ *with her* അതിങ്കൽ *with it.*
avaṅkal avaḷiṅkal atiṅkal

Plural.

	Masc. and Fem.	Neut.
1. Nom.	അവർ avar	അവ ava
		അതുകൾ atukaḷ
2. Acc.	അവരെ avare	അവയെ avaye.
		അതുകളെ atukaḷe.
3. Instr.	അവരാൽ avarāl	അവയാൽ avayāl.
		അതുകളാൽ atukaḷāl.
	അവരോട് avarōṭå	അവയോട് avayōṭå.
		അതുകളോട് atukaḷōṭå.
4. Dat.	അവർക്ക avarkkå	അവയ്ക്കു avaykkå
		അതുകൾക്കു atukaḷkkå
5. Abl.	അവരിൽനിന്ന് avarilninnå	അവയിൽനിന്ന avayilninnå.
		അതുകളിൽനിന്ന് atukaḷilninnå.
6. Gen.	അവരുടെ avaruṭe	അവയുടെ avayuṭe.
		അതുകളുടെ atukaḷuṭe.
7. Loc.	അവരിൽ avaril	അവയിൽ avayil.
		അതുകളിൽ atukaḷil.
	അവരിങ്കൽ avariṅkal	അവയിങ്കൽ avayiṅkal.

In the same way are declined :—

Demonstrative.

Masc.	Fem.	Neut.
ഇവൻ ivan	ഇവൾ ivaḷ	ഇതു് itȧ, ***this person*** or ***thing.***

Interrogative.

എവൻ evan	എവൾ evaḷ	ഏതു് ētȧ, ***which person*** or ***thing.***
		എന്തു് entȧ, ***what thing.***

The interrogative ആർ ār, ***who,*** is used for both masculine and feminine, and for both numbers.

The Reflexive Pronoun താൻ tān (pl. താങ്ങൾ tāṅṅaḷ, തങ്ങൾ taṅṅaḷ) *self,* is shortened to തൻ tan in the oblique cases, as, Acc. sing. തന്നെ tanne, (pl. തങ്ങളെ taṅṅaḷe), Dat. തനിക്കു് tanikkȧ, etc.

The Distributive Pronouns, *each*, etc., are expressed by doubling the pronouns അവൻ avan, അവൾ avaḷ, അതു് atȧ, and താൻ tān ; as, അവനവന്റെ avanavanṟe, *of each person* masc. ; താന്താൻ ചെയ്യുന്ന കർമ്മം tāntān ceyyunna karmam, *the action each one does.*

ADJECTIVES.

(*a*) Attributive words are not declined, and are placed before the nouns they qualify, as in English. These are the inflectional bases of nouns, or verbal roots, or adjectives and relative participles ; e.g. വീട്ടുപട്ടി vīṭṭu paṭṭi, *a house dog ;*

---

* This is the inflectional base of വീടു്. vīṭȧ. Nouns ending in am may, instead of following this rule, merely drop the final m, e.g. മരപ്പലക mara-ppalaka *a wooden board.*

കാഞ്ഞവെള്ളം kāñña veḷḷam, *lukewarm water;* വലിയ വീടുകൾ valiya vīṭukaḷ, *big houses;* ചെറുപയറ് ceṟu payaṟa, *small peas.*

(*b*) The Demonstrative Adjective ആ ā, *that, those,* ഈ ī, *this, these,* and the Interrogative Adjective ഏതു ētȧ, *which,* എന്തു entȧ, *what?* are also indeclinable; as, ആ കുട്ടികളുടെ ākuṭṭikaḷuṭe, *of those children.* In the same way are used the prefixes a, i, e, respectively to point out things at a distance, things near, and to ask a question.

(*c*) The past relative participle (see below, page 117) of ആ ā, *to be, to become,* namely ആയ āya added to any noun will put this noun in attributive relation to the one following; as, മിടുക്കനായ ചെറുക്കൻ miṭukkanāya ceṟukkan, *a clever boy,* കഷ്ടമായ കാര്യം kaṣṭam-āya kāryam, *a pitiable thing.* So also ഭ്രാന്തനായ ജോർജു brāntanāya jōṟjȧ, *George the mad(man,)* and ജോർജെന്ന ഭ്രാന്തൻ jōṟjenna brāntan, *the mad man who is called George* (enna being the past relative participle of the obsolete verb, en *to say* or *to call.*

The relative participles ഉള്ള uḷḷa, *containing, possessing within itself,* അല്ലാത്ത allātta, and ഇല്ലാത്ത illātta (from അൽ al, ഇൽ il, roots of negation), are added to nouns to form adjectives in the same way as āya. ulla and āya, have the same difference of meaning as their negatives illātta and allātta; e.g. മര്യാദയുള്ള കുട്ടി maryāda-y-uḷḷa kuṭṭi, *a child which has politeness;* മര്യാദആയ നടത്ത maryāda-āya naṭatta, *conduct which is polite;* മര്യാദ ഇല്ലാത്ത മനുഷ്യൻ maryāda-illātta manuṣyan, *a man who has no politeness,* മര്യാദ അല്ലാത്ത വാക്കു maryāda-allātta vākkȧ, *word which is not polite.*

DERIVATIVE NOUNS.

From primitive stems of nouns, adjectives and verbs, Derivative Nouns in frequent use are formed by the addition of suffixes :—

(*a*) മ ma, പ്പ് ppá, ത്തം ttam ച്ചം ccam പ്പം ppam, etc., the English *-ness* or *-hood* ; as, നന്മ nanma, *goodness*, വെളുപ്പ് veḷuppa, *whiteness*, വങ്കത്തം vaṅkattam, *foolishness*, തെളിച്ചം teḷiccam, *clearness*, വലുപ്പം valuppam, *bigness*, etc. (See also Verbal Nouns, page 121).

(*b*) വാൻ vān, മാൻ mān, കാരൻ kāran, etc.; as ഭാഗ്യവാൻ bāg'yavān, *a lucky person*, ശക്തിമാൻ śak'timān, *a strong man*, തോട്ടക്കാരൻ tōṭṭakkāran, *a gardener*, etc.

(*c*) The forms of the personal pronouns of the third person namely :—

	Sing.	Plur.
Masc.	അവൻ, അൻ, ആൻ, ഓൻ avan, an, ān, ōn	അവർ, അർ, ആർ, ഓർ avar ar ār ōr
Fem.	അവൾ, അൾ, ആൾ, ഓൾ aval al āl ōl	
Neut.	അത്, ത് atá tá	അവ, അതുകൾ ava atukaḷ

ceṟu, ceṟiya—*small*.

Sing.	Masc.	ceṟiyavan, *a small man*.
	Fem.	ceṟiyavaḷ, *a small woman*.
	Neut.	ceṟutá, ceṟiyatá, *a small thing*.
Plur.	Masc. and Fem.	ചെറിയവർ *small persons*. ceṟiyavar

Neut. ചെറുതുകൾ *small things.*
cerutukal,
ചെറിയവ
ceriyava
ചെറിയതുകൾ
ceriyatukal

From the adjectives എല്ലാ ellā, and സകല sakala, both meaning *all*, are formed the nouns എല്ലാവർ, എല്ലാം ellāvar, ellām, *all people, all things*, സകലർ sakalar, *all people*, and സകലതു sakalatȧ സകലം sakalam, *all things*. These being words expressing universality, take the affix ഉം um; as സകലവും sakalavum, സകലതും sakalatum, *all things*, എല്ലാവരുടേയും ellāvaruṭē-y-um, *of all people*. When they are adjectives the affix um is added to the noun which they qualify; as, എല്ലാ കുട്ടികളും, ellā kuṭṭi-kaḷum, *all children*; സകല കാൎയ്യങ്ങൾക്കും sakala kāryan-ṅaḷkkum, *for all matters*.

THE NUMERALS.

For the Cardinals, with their Malayāḷam characters, and adjectival forms, see Vocabularies.

Ordinals.

Ordinals are formed by the addition of ആം, ām, or ആമത്തെ āmatte, to the cardinals. ഒന്ന onnȧ, has an irregular ordinal ആദ്യത്തെ ādyatte, *first*, as well. These forms are used only as adjectives; as അഞ്ചാം പാഠം añcām pāṭam, *the fifth lesson*, രണ്ടാമത്തെ തവണ raṇṭāmatte tavaṇa, *the second occasion*. The adverbs *firstly, secondly*, etc., are formed by the addition of ആമത് with or without the past participle ആയി of the verb ആ *to be*; as, നാലാമത്, നിങ്ങൾ നല്ലവണ്ണം പഠിക്കണം nālāmatȧ niṅṅaḷ nallavaṇṇam paṭikkaṇam, *fourthly, you must study well ;* അവൻ നാലാമതായി വന്നു avan nālāmatāyi vannu, *He came fourth.*

By prefixing the short adjectival forms of the numbers up to five, Distributives are formed ; in the cases of ഒന്ന് onnȧ the initial vowel is lengthened ; രണ്ട് takes an initial ഈ ī ; thus:—

ഓരോന്നു ōrōnnu, *one by one.*

ഈരണ്ട് īraṇṭȧ, *two by two, in twos.*

മുമ്മൂന്ന് mummūnnȧ, *three by three.*

നന്നാല് nannālȧ, *by fours.*

ഐയ്യഞ്ച് അയ്യഞ്ച് aiyañcȧ, ayyañcȧ, *by fives.*

In the case of the other numbers, distributives are got by duplication ; thus ആറാറ് āṟāṟȧ, *by sixes ;* but പതിപ്പത്ത് patippattȧ, *by tens.* (See also vocabularies, page 61/63).

Fractions.

$\frac{1}{80}$	കാണി kāṇi	$\frac{3}{20}$	മൂന്നുമാ mūnnȧmā
$\frac{3}{80}$	മുക്കാണി mukkāṇi	$\frac{4}{20}$ or $\frac{1}{5}$	നാലുമാ nālȧmā.
$\frac{1}{20}$	മാ mā; $\frac{1}{40}$ അരമാ aramā	$\frac{1}{8}$	അരക്കാൽ arakkāl.
$\frac{1}{16}$	മാകാണി mākāṇi	$\frac{1}{4}$	ı കാൽ kāl.
$\frac{2}{20}$ or $\frac{1}{10}$	രണ്ടുമാ raṇṭȧmā	$\frac{1}{2}$	ൾ, ıı അര ara.
	ഇരുമാ irumā	$\frac{3}{4}$	ııı മുക്കാൽ mukkāl.
$\frac{3}{16}$	മുണ്ടാണി muṇṭāṇi		

N.B.—In mixed fractions, as $1\frac{1}{2}$, the final u of the numeral is dropped before അര ara, and is changed into ē before all the other fractions ; thus onnu + ara = onnara, $1\frac{1}{2}$, and onnȧ + arakkāl-onnēyarakkāl, $1\frac{1}{8}$, not, or arakkāl, which would mean $\frac{1}{8}$.

RULES OF EUPHONY.

"Euphony," says F. P. Luigi Josa,* "is a tyrant for the sake of which the Hindu sacrifices much"; but it should be added that its tyranny consists in demanding rigid adherence to set rules, most of them imperfectly known, because as yet imperfectly analysed, rather than in arbitrarily dispensing with any rules at all.

A careful study of this section will, it is hoped, explain away many apparent irregularities that puzzle and confuse would-be learners of Malayāḷam.

The Phonetic Classification of sounds is given in the following table :—

* Introductory Manual of the Hindi Language.

		Gutturals.	Palatals.	Labials.	Cerebrals.	Dentals.	Palatal-Gutturals.	Labial-Gutturals.
Vowels	Short - -	a[2]	a[3] / i	u	ṛ	ḷ	e	o
							— ai	— au
	Long - -	ā	ī	ū			ē	ō
Semi-Vowels[1]			y	m	r ṛ / ḷ / ṛ / ṇ	l / n[6]		
Consonants	Hard - -	k	c	p	ṭ	t		
	,, (aspirated)	**k**	**c**	**p**	**ṭ**	**t**		
	Soft - -	g	j	b	d	d		
	,, (aspirated)	**g**	**j**	**b**	**ḍ**	**d**		
	Nasal - -	ṅ	ñ	—[4]	—[4]	n[5]		
	Other sounds -	h	s′	v[7]	ṣ	s		

[*Remarks*—

REMARKS.

[1] Or half-consonants. These can stand by themselves at the end of words.

[2] Phonetic Sign " u ". (See page 9.)

[3] Phonetic Sign " a ". (See page 9.)

[4] These nasals are classed with the semi-vowels, because they can end words.

[5] Phonetic Sign " n′ ". (See page 11.)

[6] Phonetic Sign " n ". (See page 11.) This sound is strictly intermediate between cerebral and palatal.

[7] Usually classed as a semi-vowel, but does not end any word.

The combination of two or more words, or the component parts of a component word, or of root and termination is often attended by Euphonic changes, which may be classified under the following four heads :—

(i) Elision or dropping of a sound.

(ii) Replacement of one sound by another.

(iii) Insertion of an increment or new sound.

(iv) Duplication or doubling of a sound.

Examples of Elision.

(*a*) The final " u " of Malayāḷam words, with the exception of verbs in the past tense and certain proper nouns is replaced by " ả " (see page 9). This sound is elided whenever followed by a vowel. The reverse process happens when the following letter is a consonant, the " ả " being sounded like a full " u "
e.g., muḷakả + ari = muḷakari = *capsicum seed.*
muḷakả + poṭi = muḷakupoṭi = *capsicum powder.*

(*b*) The final " m " of neuter nouns, in the oblique cases (see page 68, *c.* (1)).

(*c*) The final " u " of finite verbs when followed by a vowel, *e.g.*—

pōkunnu + illa = pōkunnilla (*does not go*).

Examples of Replacement.

(*d*) Dentals in combination with palatals change into palatals; with cerebrals into cerebrals; a hard dental being replaced by the corresponding hard sound, and a nasal by a nasal.

(*e*) If a nasal is followed by the hard initial of a termination the latter is replaced by the same kind of sound as the nasal (*i.e.*, a palatal nasal requires the following hard sound to be palatal) and is in general further replaced by a nasal sound. The effect is to duplicate the nasal sound.

(*f*) Inflectional euphonic increments of verbs, which are dental, change their character to suit the nature of the preceding sound if these are palatal or cerebral. For examples of (*d*), (*e*), and (*f*) see sections on verbs.

Examples of Insertion.

(*g*) To prevent hiatus between two vowels, "y" or "v" is inserted, the former after a palatal vowel, and the latter after a labial vowel. In the case of gutteral vowels, the initial vowel of the second word, usually palatal or labial, determines whether "y" or "v" is to be inserted, *e.g.*—

piṭi + āna = piṭiyāna (*she elephant*)
ceytu + eṇ'ṇ'ā = ceytuveṇ'ṇ'ā (*that* (*he*) *did*)
ara + annam = arayannam (*swan*)
tī + uṇṭākku = tīyuṇṭākku (*make a fire*)
pū + illa = pūvilla (*there are no flowers*).

(*h*) A palatal sound followed by a termination beginning with "k" or the euphonic increment "kk" requires the insertion of "y" in between, at least in pronunciation,*
e.g.— ava + kku = ava(y)kku (*to them*)
vaḷa + kk + um = vaḷa(y)kkum (*will bend*).

(*i*) In certain compounds a nasal is inserted before the surd which begins the second part of the compound (see rule "*l*" following), *e.g.*—

kari + tuṇi = kari-n'-tuni (*a black cloth*)
mala + pani = mala-m-pani (*malaria*).

---

* That is to say, the "y" is sometimes written and sometimes not, but is always pronounced.

(*j*) As no Malayāḷam word can end in a "pure consonant," the half "u" (represented by "ả" in our scheme of transliteration) is inserted at the end of all words whose roots end in consonants, *e.g.*—

vayas = vayassả (*old age, age*)
pākk = pākkả (*betel-nut*)
uruk = urukả (*to melt*).

In the case of words ending in semi-vowels or "half-consonants" (see table on page 00), there are, naturally, two forms:—

pāl = pāl *or* pālả (*milk*)
payaṟ = payaṟ *or* payaṟả (*peas*)
tōḷ = tōḷ *or* tōḷả (*shoulder*).

(*k*) "tt," "in" are two euphonic increments used in oblique cases of nouns; "kk" is one used in the conjugation of verbs, and also in oblique cases of nouns. The uses of these are illustrated in the sections on nouns and verbs respectively.

Examples of Duplication.

(*l*) A surd* beginning the second half of a compound word is duplicated, except when the first word ends in a nasal:—

cīra + kūṭṭān = cīra-k-kūṭṭān (*spinach curry*)
aṟakka + poṭi = aṟakka-p-poṭi (*sawdust*)
pū + caṭṭi = pū-c-caṭṭi (*flower pot*)
peṭṭa + tala = peṭṭa-t-tala (*bald head*):
But, koṭum + kāṟṟả = koṭuṅkāṟṟả (*tempest*)
maṇ + pātṟam = maṇpātṟam (*earthen vessel*)
mun + tuṇi = mun'tuṇi (*pinafore*).

(*m*) There is no duplication in the following cases:—

(i) Plurals of enumeration, *e.g.*—
kai + kālukaḷ = kaikālukaḷ (*hand, leg*, etc., i.e., *limbs*).

---

* *i.e.*, one of the hard sounds, k, c, p, ṭ, t. This is because these letters have two sounds, one when initial and another when medial (see pp. 9-11). The preservation of the initial sound by duplication helps in the identification of the component parts of the compound.

(ii) Compounds borrowed from Sanskrit, *e.g.*—
bakṣaṇa + padārtam = bakṣaṇapadārtam (*an article of food*).

(iii) Compounds of which the first part is the root of a verb, or the second part is a verbal noun which is identical with the root of the verb, *e.g.*—
ara + kallȧ = arakallȧ (*grinding stone*)
kotukaṭi = kotukaṭi (*bite of a mosquito*).

(iv) Compounds of which the first part ends in the half "u" referred to in rule (*j*), *e.g.*—
urukkȧ + katti = urukkukatti (*steel knife*)
kaṇṇȧ + kāṇāyma = kaṇṇukāṇāyma (*blindness*).

In these cases rule (*a*) applies.

(*n*) In the cases of non-compounds, duplication is required of surds following—

(i) All case endings except those of the ablatives of connection and place, and the genitive (see page 67).

(ii) Verbs in the subjunctive mood* (see page 126).

(iii) Past adverbial participles of verbs forming their past tense in ഇ (*i*),

e.g.—(i) avane + kaṇṭu = avane-k-kaṇṭu (*I*) *saw him*

(ii) ceytāl + kāṇām = ceytāl-k-kānām (*you*) *shall see if you do* (*it*)

(iii) ōṭi + pōyi = ōṭi-p-pōyi (*ran and went*, i.e., *ran away*).

---

* It will be observed that these end in "āl" and "kil." *Cf.* the instrumental and locative above.

VERBS.

Malayāḷam Verbs may be divided into two classes, here designated "Regular" and "Irregular" for the sake of convenience.

By "Regular" Verbs is here meant Verbs that involve no euphonic insertions prior to the addition of tense terminations; by "Irregular," those that do involve such insertions, in accordance with the Rules of Euphony, of which a sketch has been given on pp. 77-81.

It is therefore reiterated that the terms are here employed in the special sense explained above. Real irregularities will be specially mentioned as they appear.

TENSE TERMINATIONS.

The primary tense terminations are those of the future and the past. The future termination is ഉ "um," and is of universal applicability.

The past terminations are ഇ "i," or ടു "tu."

In Malayāḷam, the present tense is treated as the Past of the Future, which is certainly logical enough. Thus by adding the past termination ടു "tu," to the future termination ഉം "um," we get the present termination :—

ഉം ടു umtu
= ഉന്റു un'tu (*vide* page 12).
= ഉന്നു un'n'u (Rule (*e*)*).

This is the recognised form of the termination of the present tense.†

---

* All references in this section are to the Rules of Euphony on pp. 77-81.

† It is, however, replaced in Colloquial Malayāḷam by ഉണു "uṇu," and in the case of one verb, āka, āva, *to be* or *become*, āvun'n'u has become successively âvuṇu and aṇu. The final "u" of this verb has gone the way of the final "u" in many a Malayāḷam word, and the present tense in common use is "āṇá" (= *am*, *are*, or *is*).

All verbs which form their past tense in ഇ "i" are "regular"; all except a few, which take തു "tu," are "irregular." These few consist of some ending in ട് ṭà and some in semi-vowels.

"Regular" Verbs.

I. All roots ending in pure consonants, and, therefore, written and pronounced with a succeeding half-"u" (à) in accordance with rule (*j*) are regular.

Some roots ending in semi-vowels are "regular"; these will be dealt with separately in this section.

It will be seen when we deal with "irregular" verbs that the same root has a passive or intransitive meaning, when they are conjugated in one way, and an active, transitive, or causative meaning when they are conjugated after the insertion of a hard or strengthening euphonic increment. In the case of "regular" verbs, a transitive or causative form is obtained by strengthening the root itself, *i.e.*, by replacing a nasal ending by a hard ending, or a single hard sound by a double hard sound. In other cases the causative is formed by ഇ "i", or ഇപ്പി "ippi" (*vide* page 115).

In the tables following, the roots are arranged according to their meaning as (i.) Passive or Intransitive, or as (ii.) Active, Transitive, or Causative. In the third column are given certain derivative, cognate, or allied nouns.

Example of the Conjugation of a "Regular" Verb:—

ഉരുക് uruk̀à = *to melt*

Future: ഉരുകും uruk-um = *will melt*
(Elision of à in accordance with rule (*a*)).

Past: ഉരുകി uruk-i = *melted.*

Passive or Intransitive.		Active, Transitive, or Causative		Derivative, Cognate or Allied Nouns.	
Root.	Meaning.	Root.	Meaning.	Word.	Meaning.
*Amuṅṅȧ	*to get crushed or compressed*	amukkȧ	*to crush*	amukkȧ	*a crush*
ākȧ	*to be, to become*	ākkȧ	*to cause to become*		
āṭȧ	*to dance*	āṭṭȧ	*to drive* (e.g., *cattle*), *to rock a cradle or swing*	āṭṭam	*a dance*
				āṭṭȧ	*a noise with which you want to drive away an animal or an objectionable person*
		† āṭi / āṭippi	*to cause to dance*		
aṭaṅṅȧ	*to submit*	aṭakkȧ	*to conquer, to bring under subjection*	aṭakkam	*submission*
aṭuṅṅȧ	*to be in orderly arrangement*	aṭukkȧ	*to arrange*		
				iṭukkȧ / iṭuvȧ	*a crevice or space between*
iṭuṅṅȧ	*to get crushed*	iṭukkȧ	*to crush*		
iṇaṅṅȧ	*to get tame*	iṇakkȧ	*to tame*	iṇakkam	*tameness*
iraṭȧ	*to stumble*				

* Some grammarians would have it that the root is only amuṅ(ȧ), the nasal being doubled because it is followed by a vowel (a rule invented for the purpose). There is no doubt that the double nasal is the result of the replacement of a final "k" by "ṅ," in accordance with the process described in rule (*e*). The reverse process occurs in the causative, the penultimate nasal being replaced by a hard sound. *Cf.* also Tamil

† As these roots end in "i," we do not know how to conjugate them yet.

Passive or Intransitive.		Active, Transitive, or Causative		Derivative, Cognate or Allied Nouns.	
Root.	Meaning.	Root.	Meaning.	Word.	Meaning.
iḷakȧ	*to move*	iḷakkȧ	*to move*	iḷakkam	*motion*
		un'tȧ	*to push*		
uṟaṅṅȧ	*to sleep*	uṟakkȧ	*to put to sleep*	uṟakkam	*sleep*
urukȧ	*to melt*	urukkȧ	*to melt*	urukkȧ	*steel*
uṟṟȧ, iṟṟȧ	*to drip*				
ūtȧ	*to blow (as with bellows)*	ūti, ūtippi	*to cause to blow*	ūttȧ	*the blowing of a trumpet or flute*
eṯṯȧ	*to reach*	etti	*to cause to reach*		
ēṅṅȧ	*to gasp for breath*			ēkkam	*asthma*
		kāccȧ	*to fry*		
		cappȧ	*to chew*		
cāṭȧ	*to jump*	{cāṭṭȧ	*to hurl*	cāṭṭam	*a jump*
		{cāṭi, cātippi	*to cause to jump*		
		cāmpȧ	*to pump*		
		cikkȧ	*to sift*		
		{cimmȧ	*to wink, to close one's eyes*		
		{cīmpȧ			
		{cīkȧ	*to comb*	{cīppȧ	*a comb*
		{cīvȧ		{cīṟppȧ	
		eṇṇa	*to count*	eṇṇam	*a number*
		eṛutȧ	*to write*	eṛuttȧ	*a letter*
		ēkȧ	*to give, award*		

(The causative forms of transitive verbs with no corresponding intransitive forms are formed by adding " i " or " ippi " to root.)

Passive or Intransitive. Root.	Meaning.	Active, Transitive, or Causative Root.	Meaning.	Derivative, Cognate or Allied Nouns. Word.	Meaning.
		ēntȧ	*to wield (a weapon)*		
		oppȧ	*to blot*		
		ōṅṅȧ	*to aim a blow*		
oṭṭa	*to stick to, to adhere*	oṭṭi	*to cause to stick, to paste*		
ōṭȧ	*to run*	{ōṭṭȧ	*to cause to flee*		
		{ōṭi	*to cause to run*		
kalaṅṅȧ	*to become muddy*	kalakkȧ	{*to make muddy, churn*	kalakkam	*agitation*
kaṟaṅṅȧ	*to go round and round*	kaṟakkȧ	*to turn round and round*	kaṟakkam	*revolution*
kakkȧ	*to vomit*				
kattȧ	*to burn* (e.g., *a light*)	katti			
kappȧ	*to gulp*				
kāṟȧ	*to become rancid*	kāṟi	*to turn rancid*		
		kiṭṭa	*to obtain, to become possessed of*		
ciṟṟȧ	*hiss, snarl*			cīṟṟa	*the hiss (of a snake)*
cuṅṅa	*shrink*	cukkȧ	*cause to shrink*	cukkȧ	*dried ginger*
curuṅṅa	*shrink*	curukkȧ	*shorten*	curukkam	*the substance (of a story or narration)*

Passive or Intransitive. Root.	Meaning.	Active, Transitive, or Causative Root.	Meaning.	Derivative, Cognate or Allied Nouns. Word.	Meaning.
cuṟṟȧ	*go round*	cuṟṟi	*cause to go round, trouble*		
cūṇṭȧ	*point to or at*			cūṇṭal	*angling*
		coṭṭȧ	*hit with the knuckles*		
kiluṅṅȧ	*to jingle*	kilukkȧ	*to jingle*	kilukkam	*jingling*
kuluṅṅȧ	*to shake, quake*	kulukkȧ	*to shake*	kulukkam	*quaking (earthquake)*
		kiṛukkȧ	*to tap the head with the knuckles*		
kuṭuṅṅȧ	*to get entangled*	kuṭukkȧ	*to entangle*	kuṭukkam	*entanglement*
		kuttȧ	*to stab*	kuttȧ	*a stab*
{kūkȧ / kūvȧ}	*to crow*	kūkkȧ	*to halloo*		
		kūppȧ	*to fold palms together in worship*		
kūṭȧ	*to increase*	kūṭṭȧ	*to add, join, increase*	kūṭṭam	*a crowd*
		keṭṭȧ	*to tie*	keṭṭȧ	*a bundle, a packet*
		kokkȧ	*to hook*	{kokkȧ / kokki}	*a hook*
koñcȧ	*to be playful, to prattle, to flirt*	koñci	*to indulge*	{koñcal	*babyish prattling, flirtation*
				koññanam}	*a grimace*

Passive or Intransitive. Root.	Meaning.	Active, Transitive, or Causative Root.	Meaning.	Derivative, Cognate or Allied Nouns. Word.	Meaning.
		kottȧ	*to peck, to chop*		
		koṭṭȧ	*to beat* (e.g., *a drum or gong*)		
kōṭȧ	*to go out of shape*	kōṭṭȧ	*to distort*	kōṭṭam	*defect, distortion*
ñeṭṭȧ	*to shudder*				
ñiḷaṅṅȧ	*to get crumpled or crushed* (e.g., *metal-ware*)	ñiḷakkȧ	*to crumple or crush*		
ñeṅṅȧ	*to get crushed*	ñekkȧ	*to crush, strangle*		
taṅṅȧ	*to stick to or by*	takkȧ	*to stick, to make fit*		
		tāṅṅa	*to support*		
taṭṭȧ	*to beat against*	taṭṭȧ	*to beat*		
tappȧ	*to grope for*				
taṛakȧ	*to get used to*	taṛakkȧ	*to train*	taṛakkam	*training, experience*
tiṅṅȧ	*to be crowded*	tikkȧ	*to jostle, to crowd*	tikkȧ	*crowdir g, jostling*
		tirukȧ	*to push in, screw in*	tirukȧ	*a screw*
		tiruttȧ	*to correct* (e.g., *a manuscript*)	tirutta	*fair copy*
		tīṇṭȧ	*to pollute by approach*		
tuppȧ	*to spit*				
		tuṇṇȧ	*to knit*		
tummȧ	*to sneeze*	tummi	*to cause to sneeze*		

Passive or Intransitive.		Active, Transitive, or Causative		Derivative, Cognate or Allied Nouns.	
Root.	Meaning.	Root.	Meaning.	Word.	Meaning.
		tūkȧ / tūvȧ	*to scatter*		
tūṅṅȧ	*to hang*	tūkkȧ	*to hang, to weigh*	tūkkam	*weight*
tūṟȧ	*to excrete*	tūṟṟȧ	*to suffer from diarrhœa*	tūṟṟal	*diarrhœa*
		tekkȧ	*to ladle out*		
tēṅṅȧ	*to sob*				
teṇṭȧ	*to wander aimlessly*	teṇṭi / teṇṭippi	*to drive on the streets, to cause to wander aimlessly*	teṇṭi	*a vagabond*
		tēkȧ / tēvȧ	*to lift water from well or tank by means of a special arrangement using bullock or man-power*		
		tēṭṭȧ	*to bring up in hiccoughs*		
		tēṭȧ	*to search for*		
		nakkȧ	*to lick*		
		nampȧ	*to believe*		
		nāṭṭȧ	*to plant a flagstaff*		

Passive or Intransitive.		Active, Transitive, or Causative		Derivative, Cognate or Allied Nouns.	
Root.	Meaning.	Root.	Meaning.	Word.	Meaning.
nīṅṅȧ	*to move*	nīkkȧ	*to move*	nīkkam	*movement*
nīntȧ	*to swim*	nīnti	*to cause to swim*	nīntam	*swimming*
nuṟuṅṅȧ	*to be cut to pieces*	nuṟukkȧ	*to cut to pieces*		
		nēṭȧ	*to achieve*		
		nōkkȧ	*to look, look at, look over*	nōṭṭam	*a look, discrimination*
paruṅṅȧ	*to fumble*			paruṅṅal	*fumbling, hesitation*
paṛakȧ	*to become old, to get used to*	paṛakkȧ	*to cause to grow old, to train*	paṛakkam	*oldness, mellowness*
		{pākȧ {pāvȧ	*to sow*		
		pāṭȧ	*to sing*	pāṭṭȧ	*song*
piṇaṅṅȧ	*to get estranged, quarrel*	piṇakkȧ	*to estrange*	piṇakkam	*estrangement, quarrel*
pūṭa	*to get locked*	pūṭṭȧ	*to lock*	pūṭṭȧ	a *lock*
		pūs'ȧ	*to sprinkle over oneself, to smear*		
		peṟūkkȧ	*to gather (fallen fruit)*		
perukȧ	*to multiply*	perukkȧ	*to multiply*	{perukkam {peruppam	*product* *the square of a number*
{poṅṅȧ {pontȧ	*to rise*	{pokkȧ {ponti	*to raise*	{poṅṅaccam {pokkam	*boastfulness* *height*
poṭṭȧ	*to break*	poṭṭi	*to break*		
		potta	*to cover with the hand*		

Passive or Intransitive.		Active, Transitive, or Causative		Derivative, Cognate or Allied Nouns.	
Root.	Meaning.	Root.	Meaning.	Word.	Meaning.
* pōkā / pōvā	*to go*	pōkkā	*to cause to go*		
maṅṅā	*to get dim*				
maṭaṅṅā	*to get folded*	maṭakkā	*to fold*	maṭakkā	*a fold*
mayaṅṅā	*to be overcome* (e. g., *with faintness, sleep or love*)	mayakkā	*to throw into a stupor, to captivate*	mayakkam	*stupor, uneasy sleep*
		māṭā	*to beckon*		
†māntā	*to scratch*	māntā	*to scratch*		
		miṇṭā	*to speak, utter*		
maṇṭā	*to run*				
		miṛuṅṅā / viṛuṅṅā	*to devour*		
		mīṭṭā	*to pluck the string of a musical instrument*		
muṅṅa	*to be immersed*	mukkā	*to immerse, drown*		
mukkā	*to strain* (*oneself*)				
		muṭṭā	*to knock against*		
		muttā	*to kiss*		

* Past tense (pōki) or pōyi, due to elision of "k," which also happens with ākā, *to become*.

† The same form serves for the transitive and intransitive of this word, as in English. The causative is formed with "i" or "ippi,"

Passive or Intransitive. Root.	Meaning.	Active, Transitive, or Causative Root.	Meaning.	Derivative, Cognate or Allied Nouns. Word.	Meaning.
muṛukȧ	*to be bathed in*	muṛuki	*to cause to be immersed*		
muṟukȧ	*to become taut*	muṟukkȧ	*to tighten*		
		muṟukkȧ	*to chew betel-nut*		
mūṭȧ	*to be covered*	mūṭȧ	*to cover*		
		mūṭṭȧ	*to sew up*	mūṭṭa	*a rice bag*
mēvȧ	*to remain, to dwell*				
		mōntȧ	*to sip*		
		mottȧ	*to sip and thus pollute the vessel for another person*		
vanaṅṅa	*to pay obeisance to revere*				
vaṛukȧ	*to slip* (e.g., *from one's hand*)	vaṛukkȧ	*to slip* (e.g., *a person slips*)		
vīṅṅȧ	*to swell*	vīkkȧ	*to slap, beat, bruise*		
vikkȧ	*to stammer*				
viḷaṅṅȧ	*to shine*	viḷakkȧ	*to burnish*	viḷakkȧ	*a lamp*
vitumpȧ	*to sob*				
		vīṭṭȧ	*to repay*		
vīs'ȧ	*to blow* (e.g., *the wind*)			vis'aṟi	*a fan*
		veṭṭȧ	*to cut, hack*		
		ṟāñcȧ	*to swoop upon*		

II. Roots ending in semi-vowels are mostly "irregular," but the following are among some of the "regular" roots. It will be observed that where they are not doubled, the vowel preceding is long, and that "y" and "ṛ" do not occur in the list of endings.

The double semi-vowel is as good as a consonant in Malayāḷam, so the roots are shown with the final "ȧ."

There are also irregular verbs ending in "ṟ."

Passive or Intransitive.		Active, Transitive, or Causative		Derivative, Cognate or Allied Nouns.	
Root.	Meaning.	Root.	Meaning.	Word.	Meaning.
ūr	*to slip out*	ūr	*to withdraw*		
		kōr	*to gather up (as with a trowel)*		
cār	*to lean against*	cārttȧ	*to hang upon*		
		vār	*to gather (towards oneself)*		
āṟ	*to become cool*	āṟṟȧ	*to make cool*		
ūṟ	*to be precipitated from a solution*	ūṟṟȧ	*to precipitate, to decant*		
kīṟȧ	*to tear*	kīṟȧ	*to tear*		
{kēṟ {kayaṟ	*to ascend, climb*	{kēṟṟȧ {kayaṟṟȧ	*to load, raise up*		
		kōṟ	*to scrawl*		
cīṟ	*to snarl or hiss*	cīṟṟȧ	*to snarl or hiss*		
teṟṟȧ	*to err*	teṟṟi	*to cause to err*	teṟṟȧ	*error*

Passive or Intransitive.		Active, Transitive, or Causative		Derivative, Cognate or Allied Nouns.	
Root.	Meaning.	Root.	Meaning.	Word.	Meaning.
nāṟ	*to smell, smell foul*	nāṟṟȧ	*to sniff, to disseminate a foul smell*	nāṟṟam	*smell, bad smell*
nīṟ	*to burn to ashes*	nīṟṟȧ	*to calcinate*	nīṟȧ (nūṟȧ)	*unslaked lime*
paṟṟȧ	*to adhere*	paṟṟi	*to stick*		
		paṟṟi	*to cheat*		
pāṟ	*to scatter*	pāṟṟȧ	*to scatter*		
		pēṟ	*to bear a load*		
pōṟ	*to get scratched*				
māṟ	*to change*	māṟṟȧ	*to change, to shift*	māṟṟam	*a change*
		mōṟ	*to wash up*		
vaṟṟȧ	*to dry up*	vaṟṟi	*to evaporate*	vaṟṟal	*boiled vegetable sun-dried for preserving*
		eṟṟȧ	*to release a stone from a sling*		
ēṟ	*to ascend, climb up*	ēṟṟȧ	*to load*		
		tallȧ	*to slap, beat*	tallȧ	*a slap*
		aruḷ	*to proclaim*		
āḷ	*to flare up*	āḷi	*to cause to flare up*		
		taḷḷȧ	*to push*	taḷḷȧ	*a push*
pāḷ	*to glance off* (e.g., *a knife*)				
muḷḷȧ	*to urinate*				
mūḷ	*to hum*				
minnȧ	*to shine, glitter*			minnal	*lightning*

III. The following verbs are "regular," but form their past tense with து "tu":—

Root.	Meaning.	Future.	Past.	Causative.
uṛ	*to plough*	uṛ-um	uṛ-u-tu	uṛi
ey	*to shoot with an arrow*	ey-y-um	ey-tu	eyyi eyyippi
koy	*to reap, harvest*	koy-y-um	koy-tu	koyyi koyyippi
cey	*to do*	cey-y-um	cey-tu	ceyyi ceyyippi
ney	*to weave*	ney-y-um	ney-tu	neyyi neyyippi
pey	*to rain*	pey-y-um	pey-tu	peyyi peyyippi
toṛ	*to worship*	toṛ-um	toṛ-u-tu	toṛi
paṇi	*to work*	paṇi-y-um	paṇi-tu	paṇiyi paṇiyippi

The reader cannot but be struck with the ideas conveyed by the above roots. One is driven to speculate that these were some of the oldest roots in the language, whose conjugation, being of universal concern, escaped the euphonic pedantries to which the irregular verbs became subjected.

The last root appears to have strayed into the list because of its meaning. As a matter of fact, it has an equally common past tense formed in the "irregular" way.

IV. The following verbs ending in ட் ṭ à are also regular, *i.e.*, take no inflectional increment, but the addition of து tu in the past tense results in tu being replaced by ṭu in accordance with rule (*d*). Thus —

இட் iṭà = *to put*. Future இடு iṭum

Past: இட் + து iṭ + tu
= இட் + டு iṭ + ṭu
= இட்டு iṭṭu, which is the final form.

Meaning.	Root.	Causative.	Derived, etc., and Remarks.
to go out, to be extinguished	keṭá	keṭuttá	(=*to extinguish or to spoil*)
to feel hot, to heat, to burn up	cuṭá	cuṭiyi	cūṭá =*heat*
to touch	toṭá	toṭiyi	
to plant	naṭá	naṭiyi	
to be acted on by, to be enmeshed	peṭá	peṭutta	(=*to trap*)
to put	pōṭá		
to leave	viṭá	viṭuttá.	

V. The following verbs ending in semi-vowels are also regular, *i.e.*, take no inflectional "increment," but the addition of ൟ tu in the past tense results in the "t" in the tu being replaced by the euphonic cognate of the sound ending the root, thus:—

(i) aṟ (*to be severed*) Future: aṟ-um
Past: aṟ+tu=aṟṟu

(ṟ being its own cognate). The causative form is aṟu (see p. 000 following). Similarly—

(ii) peṟ, *to give birth to* (from which we have the derived noun, pēṟá=*delivery*).

(iii) uṇ (*to eat, to dine*). Future: uṇ-ṇ-um*
Past: uṇ+tu=uṇṭu

(t being replaced by ṭ, the cognate of ṇ). The causative form is ūṭṭá=*to feed*, and a derived noun is ūṇ=*a meal.*

(iv) kāṇ=*to see.* Future: kāṇ-um
Past: kaṇ+tu=kaṇṭu† (as above).

The causative is kāṭṭá=*to show*, the root is derived from kaṇ=*the eye*, and the derived noun, kāṟcca means *vision, sight.*

---

* Inasmuch as the final ṇ is duplicated, the future tense is irregular.

† Note, however, that the vowel is shortened in the past tense, which is kaṇṭu, not kāṇṭu.

(v) tin=*to eat* Future: tin-n-um*

Past: tin-tu=tin'n'u.

The causative is tiṟṟȧ=*to feed*, and a derived noun is tiṟṟȧ=*a meal*.

---

* Inasmuch as the final "n" is duplicated, the future is irregular.

"Irregular" Verbs.

All roots ending in vowels,* and most ending in semi-vowels are "irregular" in the sense defined at the beginning of this section. They require in every case the insertion of an inflectional† euphonic increment before adding the past termination, which is ടു tu, and active, transitive, or causative roots require an increment in the future tense as

---

* The apparent exceptions often quoted, viz., ā, *to be*, and pō, *to go*, are really colloquial, or at the most commonly accepted, contractions of ākȧ and pōkȧ. The medial "k" is often treated very unceremoniously in Malayāḷam, often replaced by "v," and colloquially, by a sound hardly distinguishable from "a" itself in quick enunciation. Neither the future form ām, nor the imperative pō are tests as to what the roots are, since these may as well be the mutilated remains of ākum and pōkȧ. A clue as to what the roots are is given by the causatives. These, ākkȧ and pōkkȧ, respectively point to the roots being ākȧ and pōkȧ.

As to the unceremonious treatment of medial "k," *cf.* the contraction of makan (*son*) to mōn, exactly as avan (*he*) is contracted to ōn.

† As distinct from the universal euphonic increments "y" and "v" inserted to prevent hiatus. These latter can occur in the middle of a compound word or between two separate words in continuous enunciation. The inflectional increments of course occur only in the inflection of words.

well. The past tense increments are further modified in accordance with rules (*d*), (*e*), and (*f*) on p. 79.

There are several roots, as in English, which have a passive-intransitive, as well as an active-transitive-causative significance. But whereas in English, these are conjugated in the same way in either sense, the method of conjugation determines the sense of the Malayāḷaṃ root.

A passive-intransitive root takes no inflectional increment before the future termination ഉം um; and takes a soft, or nasal increment ന് n before the past termination തു tu. This may be called for convenience the Weak Conjugation.

An active-transitive-causative root takes a hard increment ക്ക് kk before the future, and a hard increment ത് t before the past termination. This may be called for convenience the Strong Conjugation.

As already suggested, modifications depending upon the nature of the final sound of the root ensue, hence we proceed to consider separately—

I. Roots ending in palatal vowels or semi-vowels.
II. Roots ending in other vowels.
III. Roots ending in other semi-vowels.

Conjugation of a Weak Irregular Verb ending in a Palatal:

കരി kari = *to get burnt*

Future കരിയും kari-y-um = *will get burnt* (i)

Insertion of " y " in accordance with rule (*g*)

Past : കരി + ന് + തു kari + n + tu

= കരി + ഞ് + തു kari + ñ + tu (rule (*f*))

= കരി + ഞ് + ചു kari + ñ + cu (rule (*e*))

= കരി + ഞ് + ഞു kari + ñ + ñu (rule (*e*))

= കരിഞ്ഞു kariññu = *got burnt* (ii)

(i) and (ii) are the final forms of the future and past tenses after euphony has done her worst.

Conjugation of a Strong Irregular Verb.

കരി kari = *to burn, char*

Future: കരി + ക്ക് + ഉം	kari + kk + um
= കരി + (യ്) + ക്കും	kari + y + kkum (rule (*h*))
= കരിയ്ക്കും	kari(y)kkum = *will burn*
Past: കരി + ത് + തു	kari + t + tu
= കരി + ച് + തു	kari + c + tu (rule (*f*))
= കരി + ച് + ചു	kari + c + cu (*rule* (*d*))
= കരിച്ചു	kariccu = *burnt*.

The last line in each case is the final form of the future and past tenses.

To this class belongs all roots derived from Malayāḷam nouns or verbs, (*e.g.*, those causatives of "regular" verbs that end in "i" or "ippi," as well as the roots borrowed from Sanskrit which are Malayāḷamized by the addition of "i." All these derived verbs are conjugated strongly, and find no place in the list below except incidentally.

I. Irregular Verbs ending in Palatals :—PALATAL "A."

MEANING	ROOT. Weak Conjugation	ROOT. Strong Conjugation	Meaning when different from Column (1)	Derivative, Cognate and Allied Nouns
to shut	aṭa	aṭa		aṭappà = *a lid*
to come close or near, to go out (as a fire or light)	aṇa	aṇa	*to hold close, to embrace to extinguish*	aṇa = *a dam across a river*
		aya	*to send*	
to get ground or crushed	ara	ara	*to grind, to crush*	aravà = *consistency of paste obtained by grinding,* e.g., *of curry paste*
to wander aimlessly	ala	ala	*to come and strike against through aimless wandering*	ala = *a wave*

Palatal "A"—*continued.*

MEANING	ROOT Weak Conjugation	ROOT. Strong Conjugation	Meaning when different from Column (1)	Derivative, Cognate and Allied Nouns
*to beat**	aṟa			
		aṟa	†*to be disgusted at*	aṟappȧ = *disgust*
to get loose or slack	aṟa	aṟa	*to slacken*	aṟa = *a clothes peg*
to break with, to quarrel, to get entangled	iṭa			
to work loose	iḷa	iḷa	*to loosen, to administer loosely, remit a fine*	
to wriggle as a snake	iṟa	iṟa	*to drag along*	
to break	uṭa	uṭa	*to break*	
to rub away	ura	ura	*to rub*	
to get crumpled	ula	ula	*to crumple*	
to solidify	uṟa	uṟa		
*to churn**	kaṭa			
to cry	kara			
to be spread apart	kava	kava	*to spread apart*	
*to lose**	kaḷa			
		kaṟa	*to ache*†	kaṟappȧ = *ache*
		kita	*to pant*†	kitappȧ—*pant*
		kiḷa	*to dig*	
		kura	*to bark or cough*	
to get mixed	kuṟa	kuṟa	*to mix*	kuṟampȧ = *an emulsion*
to fall supine	caṭa	caṭa	*to grow lean*	caṭappȧ = *leanness*
to get crushed or bruised	cata	cata	*to crush, to bruise*	catavȧ = *a bruise*

* Transitive, but conjugated weak.
† Intransitive, but conjugated strong.

Palatal "A"—*continued.*

Meaning	Root. Weak Conjugation	Root. Strong Conjugation	Meaning when different from Column (1)	Derivative, Cognate and Allied Nouns
*to get adorned, to don equipment or uniform**	cama			
to become, to be transformed	cama	cama	*to make, to create, or to transform*	
		cava	*to chew, masticate*	
		cira	*to shave*	
		cila	*to chirp*†	
		cina	*to neigh*†	
		cuma	*to cough*†	
		cuva	*to taste, taste bad*†	
*to obstruct**	taṭa			taṭavȧ = *a prison*
to get nailed against, to be impaled	taṟa	taṟa	*to rail, to impale*	
	taṛa	taṛa	*to remit (a punishment or fine)*‡	
to be sufficient	tika	tika	*to make sufficient*	
*to search**	tira			tirakkȧ = *to search or inquire is a related root*
		tiḻa	*to boil*	
		tuṭa	*to wipe*	
		tuṇa	*to protect, help*	tuṇa = *a help*
to perish	tula	tula	*to destroy*	
to row	tuṛa*			
		naṛa	*to grow grey*†	nara = *greyness*

* Transitive, but conjugated weak.
† Intransitive, but conjugated strong.
‡ This root conjugated either weakly or strongly.

Palatal "A"—*continued.*

Meaning	Root. Weak Conjugation	Root. Strong Conjugation	Meaning when different from Column (1)	Derivative, Cognate and Allied Nouns
to become wet	nana	nana	*to dampen, to water*	nanavá = *dampness*
to fill	niṟa	niṟa	*to fill*	
to lather, to foam	nura			nura = *foam*
		paka	*to be puzzled*†	
		paṭa	*to create*	
to lather, to foam	pata	pata	*to lather, to foam*	pata = *foam*
to say	paṟa			
to beat helplessly (e.g., *a bird its wings*)‡	piṭa	piṭa		
to become entangled	piṇa	piṇa	*to entangle*	
		piṟa	*to expiate*†	piṟa = *a fine, a sin*
to smoke	puka	puka	*to smoke*	
*to weave** (*a basket*)	{maṭa, meṭa			
to fall on one's back‡	mala	mala		
		mura	*to grow old*†	
	vara	vara	*to draw* (e.g., *a line or a drawing*)	
to be in distress	vala	vala	*to persecute*	
to bend	vaḷa	vaḷa	*to bend*	{vaḷavá = *curvature*, vaḷa = *a bangle*
to get sown	vita	vita	*to sow*	vittá = *seed*
		viṟa	*to shudder*†	
to sprout	viḷa			

* Transitive, but conjugated weak.
† Intransitive, but conjugated strong.
‡ This root conjugated either strongly or weakly.

PALATALS: "I," "Ī," "E" and "Y."

MEANING	ROOT. Weak Conjugation	ROOT. Strong Conjugation	Meaning when different from Column (1)	Derivative, Cognate and Allied Nouns
to beat against	aṭi	aṭi	*to beat*	
*to wear**	aṇi			
to dissolve	ali	ali	*to dissolve*	
*to cut to small pieces, to mince**	ari	ari	*to sift*	
to putrefy	aḷi	aḷi	*to cause to putrefy*	
*to know, understand**	aṟi			aṟivà = *knowledge*
to get untied	aṟi	aṟi	*to untie*	
to crumble down, cave in	iṭi	iṭi	*to beat with clenched fists*	
to be chagrined, to be forced to grin through shame	iḷi	iḷi	*to grin*	
to peal away (e.g., *the skin of snakes*)	uri	uri	*to skin, to detach fruit from a bunch, to peel*	
to burn, to taste hot	eri	eri	*to burn*	erivà = *hot taste*
		kaṭi	*to bite*	
to burn	kari	kari	*to burn*	kari = *charcoal*
*to transcend**	kavi			
		kaḷi	*to play*	kaḷi = *a game*
to be consumed / *to be over* / *to be able*	kaṟi	kaṟi	*to consume* / *to finish*	
to become less	kiṟi	kiṟi	*to subtract*	
		kuṭi	*to drink*	kuṭi = *a drink*
		kuḷi	*to bathe*	kuḷi = *a bath*
		kuṟi	*to note, indicate, point to*	
		kuḻi	*to dig (a pit)*	kuḻi = *a pit*

* Transitive, but conjugated weak.

Palatal: "I," "Ī," "Ē," and "Y."—*continued.*

MEANING	ROOT. Weak Conjugation	ROOT. Strong Conjugation	Meaning when different from Column (1)	Derivative, Cognate and Allied Nouns
		cati	*to cheat*	
		ciri	*to laugh*	
to become bad	cī	cī	*to spoil*	
*to scour**	curi			curika = *a weapon*
to get wrinkled or crumpled	cuḷi	cuḷi	*to crumple*	culivȧ = *a crease*; cuḷi
to lean	ceri	ceri	*to tilt*	cerivȧ = *slope*
*to pour down, to scatter in profusion**	cori			
		taṭi	*to become fat*†	taṭi = *obesity*
		tari	*to tingle*	tarippa = *tinglin*
to set in a glare	tuṟi	tuṟi	*to glare, stare*	
to rub, to wear away, to be covered	tē	tē	*to rub, to smear*	
to stick to	pati	pati	*to stick*	
to fall down (e.g., fruit from its stem)	paṟi	paṟi	*to pluck*	
		paṟi	*to incriminate, accuse, slander*	paṟi = *slander*
		piṭi	*to catch, to hold*	piṭi = *grip, a hand*
to get entwined, to spin round and round	piri	piri	*to entwine, to spin a rope)*	piri = *a screw*
to leave (a person)	piri	piri	*to separate, to dismiss*	

* Transitive, but conjugated weak.
† Intransitive, but conjugated strong.

Palatals: "I," "I," "E" and "Y"—*continued.*

MEANING	ROOT. Weak Conjugation	ROOT. Strong Conjugation	Meaning when different from Column (1)	Derivative, Cognate and Allied Nouns
to crumble to powder	poṭi	poṭi	*to powder*	poṭi = *powder, dust, snuff*
to pack (in a parcel)*	poti	poti	*to unhusk (a cocoanut)*	poti = *a parcel*
to fry	pori	pori	*to fry*	pori = *fried (rice) grain*
		mari	*to die*†	(from Sanskrit)
		maṭi	*to be lazy, to hesitate*†	
to be opened wide (the eyes)	miṛi	miṛi	*to open one's eyes wide*	miṛi = *the pupil of the eye*
to perish, to be ruined	muṭi	muṭi	*to ruin*	
to be cut	muṟi	muṟi	*to cut*	muṟi = *a wound*
to have a wry face	muni			
to get crisp	mori	mori	*to fry*	
		vaṭi	*to shave clean, to rinse*	
to become taut	vali	vali	*to draw, to pull*	
to spread	viri	viri	*to spread*	
		viḷi	*to call*	
to discard, to forsake*	veṭi			
to gather momentum as for a blow*	āy			
to become warm	kāy	kāy	*to fructify*	
to lean against, to bend down	cāy	cāy	*to bend down*	
		tay	*to beat*	
to flee	pāy	pāy	*to cause to flee*	
to fade, to be rubbed away	māy	māy	*to rub out, rub away*	
to graze	mēy	mēy	*to graze*	
		vay / vey	*to place, to cook*	

* Transitive, but conjugated weak.

† Intransitive, but conjugated strong.

II. Irregular Verbs ending in Non-Palatal Vowels :—

The verb ചാ cā *to die*, has for the future tense ചാവും cā-v-um or ചാകും cākum. Past tense is ചത്തു ca-t-tu.

The verb വേ vē, *to burn, to get cooked*, has വേവും vē-v-um, or വേകും vē-k-um, for the future, and വെന്തു ve-n-tu for the past.

The verb നോ nō, *to be pained*, has നോവും nō -v-um for the future, and നൊന്തു no-n-tu for the past.

Verbs ending in "u," "o," or guttural "a" are all conjugated strongly in the future tense ; but in the past tense the conjugation is either strong or weak.

EXAMPLES.

ഇര ira, *to beg*
Future : ഇരക്കും ira-kk-um*
Past : ഇര + ന് + തു ira + n + tu
= ഇര + ന് + നു ira + n + nu (rule *e*).
= ഇരന്നു iranṇu (which is the final form)
കൊടു koṭu, *to give him or her*.
Future : കൊടുക്കും koṭu-kk-um
Past : കൊടു + ട് + തു koṭu + t + tu
= കൊടുത്തു koṭuttu

(*All strong in the Future Tense.*)

MEANING	ROOT. (Weak Past)	ROOT (Strong Past)	Causative	Derivative, Cognate and Allied Nouns
To approach		aṭu	aṭu-ppi	aṭuppam = *nearness*
to sever		aṟu‡		
to sit	iru†		iru-ttȧ	
to wear		uṭu	uṭu-ppi	uṭuppȧ = *dress*
to take		eṭu	eṭu-ppi	

* No incidence of "y" before "kk," as the preceding sound is non-palatal, *vide* rule page 79.

† Future correctly iru-kk-um, corrupted in speech and writing to iri-y-kkum.

‡ Causative of "aṟ," *vide* p. 96.

All strong in the Future Tense—*continued.*

MEANING.	ROOT. (Weak Past).	ROOT. (Strong Past)	Causative	Derivative, Cognate and Allied Nouns
to become black		kaṟu	kaṟu-ppi	kaṟuppá = *black colour*
to give (him, her, or them)		koṭu	koṭu-ppi	
to obstruct		taṭu	taṭu-ppi	
to feel cold		taṇu	taṇu-ppi	taṇuppá = *cold*
to blush, to glow		tuṭu	tuṭu-ppi	tuṭuppá = *blush*
to divide, share, to half		paku	paku-ppi	pakuti (pāti) } *share half*
to ripen		paṟu	paṟu-ppi	
to putrefy		puṟu	puṟu-ppi	puṟu = *a worm, a maggot*
to flower		pū		pū = *a flower*
to forbear		poṟu	poṟu-ppi	
to be surfeited		maṭu	maṭu-ppi	
to become mature		mū	mū-ppi •	mūppá = *prominence*
to fry		vaṟu	vaṟu-ppi	
to hate		veṟu	veṟu-ppi	
to fit		o	o-ppi	
to measure	aḷa		aḷa-ppi	aḷavá = *measurement*
to beg	ira		ira-ppi	
to milk	kaṟa		kaṟa-ppi	
to feel heavy		kana	kana-ppi	kanam = *weight*
to lie down	kiṭa		kiṭa-ttá	kiṭakka = *a bed*
to become red	cuva (cuma)		cuva-ppi	cuvappá = *red colour*
to bear a burden	cuma		cuma-p	cumaṭá = *a load*
to borrow	tura		tura-ppi	{ turaṅkam = *a tunnel*; turappan = *bandicoot*

All strong in the Future Tense—*continued.*

MEANING	ROOT. (Weak Past)	ROOT. (Strong Past)	Causative	Derivative, Cognate and Allied Nouns
to open	tuṟa		tuṟa-ppi	
to walk	naṭa		naṭa-ttå	naṭappå = *conduct*
to stand in a row	nira		nira-ttå	
to spread	para		para-ttå	
to fly	paṟa		paṟa-ppi	{pṟavå = *a dove* {paṟava = *a bird*
to be born	piṟa			
to smell		maṇa	maṇa-ppi	maṇam-*smell*
to forget	maṟa		maṟa-ppi	maṟavi = *forgetfulness*

III. Irregular Verbs ending in Semi-Vowels :—

It is beyond the scope of the present volume to attempt to analyse the final forms of the past tenses of all verbs ending in these troublesome sounds which, as their name indicates, behave sometimes as consonants and sometimes as vowels. Instances of their behaviour as consonants have already been given in the section on regular verbs. In the following tables the roots are classified according to their endings, and the final forms of the future and past tenses are given. Their conformity with the rules of euphony will be apparent when once it is realised that the latter are of progressive application *i.e.*, indicate stages in the evolution of the language. In certain cases the evolution is not complete, and the final form is still that which has become obsolete in the others :—

(*a*) Roots ending in r, ṟ (i.) (Weak Conjugation.)

MEANING.	ROOT.	Future Past.	Causatives and Derived Nouns, &c.
to waken	uṇar	uṇarum uṇaṟn'n'u	uṇaṟttá=*to waken.*
to get compressed	amar	amarum amaṟn'n'u	amaṟ=*to compress* (see below) amaṟttá=*to suppress, oppress*
to mix	kalar	kalarum kalaṟn'n'u	kalaṟttá=*to mix* kalaṟppá=*mixture* kalaṟcca
to rob	kavar	kavarum kavaṟn'n'u	kavaṟcca=*robbery*
to gnaw	kār	kārum kāṟn'n'u	
to join	cēr	cērum cēṟn'n'u	cēṟppá=*a joint relationship* cēṟcca
to leak	cōr	cōrum cōṟn'n'u	cōṟ=*to drain* cōṟá=*boiled rice*
to give (to me)	tar	tarum tan'n'u	
to be finished	tīr	tīrum tīṟn'n'u	tīṟ=*to finish* tīṟcca=*certainly* tīṟppá=*decision*
to continue	tuṭar	tuṭarum tuṭaṟn'n'u	tuṭaṟcca=*continuation*
to fill in	tūr	tūrum tūṟn'n'u	tūṟ=*to fill in*
to get dry	tōr	tōrum tōṟn'n'u	tōṟttá=*to dry* tōṟttá=*a towel*
to vow, an offering	n'ēr	n'ērum n'ēṟn'n'u	n'ēṟcca=*an offering*
to embrace	puṇar	puṇarum puṇaṟn'n'u	

MEANING.	ROOT.	Future Past.	Causatives and Derived Nouns, &c.
to come away	pōr	pōrum pōn'n'u	
to fall on one's back	malar	malarum malaṟn'n'u	malaṟttȧ = *to cause to fall on one's back*
to come	vaṙ	varum van'n'u	varavȧ = *arrival* varattȧ = *to cause to arrive*
to blossom, to *unfold*	viṭar	viṭarum viṭaṟn'n'u	viṭaṟttȧ = *to distend*

Roots ending in r, ṟ (Strong Conjugation.)

(ii.) Strong Conjugation.

MEANING.	ROOT.	Future Past.	Causatives and Derived Nouns, &c.
to remember	ōṟ	ōṟ-kk-um ōṟ-t-tu	ōṟma = *memory*
to taste sour	cavaṟ	cavaṟ-kk-um cavaṟ-t-tu	cavaṟppȧ = *sour-*[*ness*
*to swell up, to get bloated**	cīṟ	cīṟ-kk-um cīṟ-t-tu	
to join†	cēṟ	cēṟ-kk-um cēṟ-t-tu	
to drain†	cōṟ	cōṟ-kk-um cōṟ-t-tu	
to finish†	tīṟ	tīṟ-kk-um tīṟ-t-tu	
to fill in, to level†	tūṟ	tūṟ-kk-um tūṟ-t-tu	
to face, to oppose	n'ēṟ	n'ēṟ-kk-um n'ēṟ-t-tu	
to see	pāṟ	pāṟ-kk-um pāṟ-t-tu	
to compress†	amaṟ	amaṟ-kk-um amaṟ-t-tu	

* Intransitive, but conjugated strongly.

† Compare the weak forms.

(b) Roots ending in l. (i.) Weak Conjugation.

MEANING.	ROOT.	Future Past.	Causatives and Derived Nouns, &c.
to kill	kol	kol-l-um* kon'n'u	kolli=*to cause to kill* kola=*murder*
to go to	cel	cel-l-um* cen'n'u	
to say, to utter	col†	col-l-um* con'n'u	collȧ=*a saying*
to swing	ñāl	ñālum ñān'n'u	ñāttȧ=*to suspend from* ñāttȧ=*a nose-pendant*
to stand	n'il	n'il-l-um*‡ n'in'n'u	n'iṟtta=*to cause to stand*
to become level	n'ikal	n'ikalum n'ikan'n'u	n'ikattȧ=*to level* n'ikappȧ=*level*
to conquer	vel	vel-l-um* ven'n'u	

(ii.) Strong Conjugation.

to receive	ēl	ēl-kk-um ēṟṟu	
to get defeated§	tōl	tōl-kk-um tōṟṟu	tōlppi=*to defeat* tōlma=*defeat, failure*
to spin	n'ūl	n'ūl-kk-um n'ūṟṟu	n'ūl=*thread, yarn*
to sell	vil	vil-kk-um viṟṟu	

* Note that the ending is duplicated prior to the addition of the future termination.

† Or coll, when the conjugation is regular, viz., coll-um, coll-i.

‡ This form of the future is obsolete. The ordinary form is strong, viz., n'il-kk-um.

§ Intransitive, but conjugated strongly.

MEANING.	ROOT.	Future Past.	Causatives and Derived Nouns, &c.
		(c) Roots ending in ḷ. (i) Weak Conjugation.	
to roll	uruḷ	uruḷ-um uruṇṭu	uruṭṭȧ=*to trundle*
to gnaw	karaḷ	karaḷum karaṇṭu	
to lengthen	n'īḷ	n'īḷum n'īṇṭu	n'īṭṭa=*to lengthen* n'īḷam=*length*
to split	viḷ	viḷ-ḷum viṇṭu	
		(ii.) Strong Conjugation.	
to steal	kaḷ	kaḷ-kk-um† kaṭ-ṭu	kaḷḷam=*a lie* kaḷavȧ=*a theft*
to hear	kēḷ	kēḷ-kk-um kēṭṭu	kēḷvi=*hearing, a rumour, fame*
to marry	vēḷ	vēḷ-kk-um vēṭṭu	vēḷi=*marriage*
		(d) Roots ending in ṟ (all weak).	
to sink	āṟ	āṟ-um āṇṭu	āṟam=*depth*
to cry	kēṟ	kēṟum kēṇu	
to scour	cūṟ	cūṟum cūn'n'u	
to sink	tāṟ	tāṟum tān'n'u	tāṟttȧ=*to lower, to cause to sink* tāṟcca=*depth*
to grope under	n'ūr	n'ūṟum n'ūṇṭu, n'ūn'n'u	

† Colloquially, "kakkum."

Meaning.	Root.	Future Past.	Causatives and Derived Nouns, &c.
to be submerged	pūṛ	pūṛum pūṇṭu	pūṛttá pūttá } *to submerge*
to dwell, to reign over	vāṛ	vāṛum vāṇu	vāṛcca=*reign*
to fall	viṛ	viṛum viṇu	vīcca=*fall*
to roll over	kamiṛ	kamiṛum kamin'n'u	

For purposes of reference, the following summary of the classification of verbs on pp. 82-113 will be found useful:—

(A) Regular Verbs.

I. Roots ending in pure consonants (past tense in "i"), pp. 82-92.

II. Roots ending in semi-vowels (past tense in "i"), pp. 93-94.

III. Roots ending in semi-vowels (past tense in "tu" and no euphonic changes), p. 95.

IV. Roots ending in the consonant "ṭá" (past tense in "tu"), p. 95.

V. Roots ending in semi-vowels (past tense in "tu," with euphonic changes but no euphonic increments), pp. 96-97.

(B) Irregular Verbs.

I. Roots ending in palatal vowels and semi-vowels, pp. 99-105.

II. Roots ending in non-palatal vowels, pp. 106-108.

III. Roots ending in other semi-vowels, viz. :—

(*a*) (i) Weak Roots in r, ṛ, pp. 109.
(ii) Strong Roots in r, ṛ, p. 110.

(*b*) (i) Weak Roots in l, p. 111.
(ii) Strong Roots in l, p. 111.

(*c*) (i) Weak Roots in ḷ, p. 112.
(ii) Strong Roots in ḷ, p. 112.

(*d*) **Roots in ṛ, p. 112.**

Person, Gender and Number.

Unlike Tamil, Telugu and Canarese, Malayāḷam verbs take no terminations. to indicate person or number. Thus പോകുന്നു pōkunnu may mean (*I*) *go*, (*thou*) *goest*, (*he*, *she* or *it*) *goes*, *we go*, *you go* or *they go*. Similarly, പോയി pō'yi means merely *went* as in English, and പോകും pōkum, *shall* or *will go*. The person, number and gender are understood only from the subject of the verb.

Negative Verbs.

Negative verbs are formed by adding ആ ā to the primitive roots. The stems so formed are conjugated as weak verbs; e.g. പറ paṛa, *to say*, പറയാ paṛa-y-ā, ***not to say***.

Present.	Past	Future.
പറയായുന്നു parayāyunnu	പറയാഞ്ഞു parayāññu (underlined)	പറയാ paṛayā (underlined)
		പറയായും paṛayāyum
		പറയായ്വു paṛayāyvu.

Most of these forms are now obsolete, the underlined alone being used to any extent. The negative, now in common use, is obtained by the addition of ഇല്ല illa to the positive, present and past tenses; e.g.

ഞാൻ പറയുന്നില്ല, *I do not say.*
ñān paṟayunnilla.
ഞാൻ പറഞ്ഞില്ല, *I did not say.*
ñān paṟaññilla.

In the future tense illa is added not to the future positive, but to the verbal noun in ക* (See below, page 121)

ഞാൻ പറയുകയില്ല, *I shall not say.*
ñān paṟayukayilla.
(shortened into ñān paṟayilla ഞാൻ പറയില്ല.

Causative and Denominative Verbs.

Causative Verbs are formed in several ways ;

(*a*) Commonly, by adding ഇ i (or പി pi or പ്പി ppi) to the root. These are conjugated as strong verbs. Thus :—

അടു, *to come near*	അടുക്കുന്നു	അടുത്തു	അടുക്കും
aṭu	aṭukkunnu	aṭuttu	aṭukkum.
അടുപ്പി *to make,*	അടുപ്പിക്കുന്നു	അടുപ്പിച്ചു	അടുപ്പിക്കും
aṭuppi *to approach*	aṭuppikkunnu	aṭuppiccu	aṭuppikkum
തോല്, *to fail*	തോല്ക്കുന്നു	തോററു	തോല്ക്കും
tōl	tōlkkunnu	tōṯṯu	tōlkkum.
തോല്പി, *to defeat*	തോല്പിക്കുന്നു	തോല്പിച്ചു	തോല്പിക്കും
tōlpi	tōlpikkunnu	tōlpiccu	tōlpikkum.
കാണ്, *to see*	കാണുന്നു	കണ്ടു	കാണും
kān	kāṇunnau	kaṇṭu	kāṇum.
കാണി, *to show*	കാണിക്കുന്നു	കാണിച്ചു	കാണിക്കും
kāṇi	kāṇikkunnu	kāṇiccu	kāṇikkum

(*b*) By strengthening the root through doubling or hardening the final Consonant, or by the suffixes ത്ത് ttá, ച്ച് ccá, etc.; e.g.

* Corresponding to Tamil கை

ഓട്, *to run*	ഓടുന്നു	ഓടി	ഓടും
ōṭa	ōṭunnu	ōṭi	ōṭum.
ഓട്ടു°, *to make*	ഓട്ടുന്നു	ഓട്ടി	ഓട്ടും
ōṭṭa	ōṭṭunnu	ōṭṭi	ōṭṭum
ഇറങ്ങു°, *to descend*	ഇറങ്ങുന്നു	ഇറങ്ങി	ഇറങ്ങും
iṟaṅṅa	iṟaṅṅunnu	iṟaṅṅi	iṟaṅṅum
ഇറക്കു°, *to lower*	ഇറക്കുന്നു	ഇറക്കി	ഇറക്കും
iṟakka	iṟakkunnu	iṟakki	iṟakkum.
കട, *to cross*	കടക്കുന്നു	കടന്നു	കടക്കും
kaṭa	kaṭakkunnu	kaṭannu	kaṭakkum.
കടത്തു°, *to transport*	കടത്തുന്നു	കടത്തി	കടത്തും
kaṭatta	kaṭattunnu	kaṭatti	kaṭattum.
കാ, *to get warm*	കായുന്നു	കാഞ്ഞു	കായും
kā	kāyunnu	kāññu	kāyum.
കാച്ചു°, *to boil*	കാച്ചുന്നു	കാച്ചി	കാച്ചും
kācca	kāccunnu	kācci	kāccum.

(*c*) By converting a weak verb into a strong one in conju gation ; e.g.

അട, *to get closed*	അടയുന്നു	അടഞ്ഞു	അടയും
aṭa	aṭayunnu	aṭaññu	aṭayum.
അട, *to shut*	അടക്കുന്നു	അടച്ചു	അടക്കും
aṭa	aṭakkunnu	aṭaccu	aṭakkum.
ചത, *to get crushed*	ചതയുന്നു	ചതഞ്ഞു	ചതയും
cata	catayunnu	cataññu	catayum.
ചത, *to crush*	ചതക്കുന്നു	ചതച്ചു	ചതക്കും
cata	catakkunnu	cataccu	catakkum.
കരി, *to get burnt*	കരിയുന്നു	കരിഞ്ഞു	കരിയും
kari	kariyunnu	kariññu	kariyum.
കരി, *to scorch*	കരിക്കുന്നു	കരിച്ചു	കരിക്കും
kari	karikkunnu	kariccu	karikkum.

Denominative Verbs.

The following are a few examples of Denominative Verbs, *i.e.* verbs derived from Substantives. They are formed by the addition of the tense signs, weak or strong, to the root, with the connecting vowel ഇ i*.

Root.	Verb.	Pres.	Past.	Fut.
മരം	മരവി	മരവിക്കുന്നു	മരവിച്ചു	മരവിക്കും
maram	maravi	maravikkunnu	maraviccu	maravikkum
wood	*to be paralysed*			
കുല	കുല	കുലക്കുന്നു	കുലച്ചു	കുലക്കും
kula		kulakkunnu	kulaccu	kulakkum.
a bunch of fruit	*to fructify*			
കുഴമ്പ്	കുഴമ്പി	കുഴമ്പിക്കുന്നു	കുഴമ്പിച്ചു	കുഴമ്പിക്കും
kurampȧ	kuṛmmī	kuṛampikkunnu	kuṛampicca	kuṛampikkum
thickened fluid	*to get thick*			
തൊലി toli *skin*	തൊലി	തൊലിയുന്നു	തൊലിഞ്ഞു	തൊലിയും
	toli	toliyunnu	toliññu	toliyum.
	to get peeled			
	തൊലി	തൊലിക്കുന്നു	തൊലിച്ചു	തൊലിക്കും
	toli	tolikkunnu	toliccu	tolikkum
	to peel			

PARTICIPLES.

Participles are of two kinds, Relative and Adverbial.

(i.). The Relative Participle (പേരെച്ചം pēreccam) is a verbal adjective, with an affirmative or negative signification, standing in attributive relation to the noun following it.

* Subject, of course, to the rules of euphony.

In the affirmative its present and past forms are obtained by adding അ a to the Conjugational base, dropping the final vowel, if it be ഉ u.

Thus ഓടുന്നു ōṭunnu, the present tense of ഓടു ōṭā, *to run*, gives ഓടുന്ന ōṭunna, *who* or *which runs, running*, and ഓടി ōṭi, *ran*, gives ഓടിയ ōṭiya, *who* or *which ran*, കൊടുക്കുന്നു koṭukkunnu, *give*, gives കൊടുക്കുന്ന koṭukkunna, *who* or *which gives*; കൊടുത്തു, *gave*, gives കൊടുത്ത *who* or *which gave*; ആകുന്നു ākunnu, *become*, gives ആകുന്ന ākunna, *becoming*, ആയി āyi, *became*, gives ആയിയ āyiya, contracted to ആയ āya.

The Future form is the same as the Future Tense, thus, കുരങ്ങൻ ചാടും kuraṅṅan cāṭum, *the monkey will jump*, ചാടും കുരങ്ങൻ *the monkey, which will jump* (or *is in the habit of jumping*.

By adding ആ or ആത്ത ātta, and ആഞ്ഞ āñña respectively to the conjugational base of the Present (or the Future) tense, *i.e.*, naṭu vinayeccam, which is the same as the infinitive in അ, ക്ക, dropping its final vowel., we get three negative forms, the first two of indeterminate tense, and the last of past tense. Thus:—

അടിക്കുന്നു, *beats* aṭikkunnu അടിക്കും, *will beat* aṭikkum	അടിക്കാ aṭikkā* അടിക്കാത്ത aṭikkātta	*who* or *which does not (did not* or *will not beat)*
	അടിക്കാഞ്ഞ aṭikkāñña,	*who* or *which did not beat.*
പൊളിയുന്നു, *splits* poḷiyunnu പൊളിയും *will split* poḷiyum	പൊളിയാ poḷiyā* പൊളിയാത്ത poḷiyātta	*which does not (did not* or *will not) split.*
	പൊളിയാഞ്ഞ poḷiyāñña,	*which did not split*

---

* Used chiefly in poetry

Although this Participle qualifies nouns of any gender, number or case (just like an English adjective) without itself undergoing any change, yet it does not lose its verbal character, i.e. it has a subject, can govern an object, etc., e.g.

ഞാൻ അയാളോട് പറഞ്ഞ സംഗതി

ñān ayāḷōṭá paraññа samgati

The thing that I told him.

അവൻ പോയ സ്ഥലം

avan pōya stalam.

The place that he went to.

Besides, its sense might be active or passive, e.g.

ആന പൊട്ടിച്ച ചങ്ങല, *The chain that the elephant broke.*

āna poṭṭicca caññala.

ചങ്ങല പൊട്ടിച്ച ആന, *The elephant that broke (its) chain*

caṅṅala poṭṭicca āna.

(ii.). The Adverbial Participle (വിനയെച്ചം vinayeccam- is widely used in Malayāḷam constructions, and may be sub. divided into three classes; the മുൻവിനയെച്ചം munvinayeccam (or past adverbial participle); the പിൻവിനയെച്ചം. piunvinayeccam (or the Infinitive of Purpose) and the നടുവിനയെച്ചം (or the Dravidian Infinitive). (See Infinitive Mood, page 122).

The Past Adverbial Participle has also affirmative and negative forms.

A. The former is formed by changing the final ഉ u of the past tense into ് á; where the past tense is formed in ഇ i, the participle and the verb in the past tense are the same in form. Thus:—

കളഞ്ഞു, *lost* കളഞ്ഞ്; *having lost.*

kaḷaññu kaḷaññá

ഓടി, *ran* or *having ran.*

ōṭi

The increment ഇട്ടു് iṭṭȧ, itself the past adverbial participle of the auxiliary ഇടു് iṭȧ, *to put*, is often used to strengthen the past adverbial participle of verbs :—thus കളഞ്ഞിട്ടു് kaḷaññiṭṭȧ, *having lost*, ഓടിയിട്ടു് oṭiyiṭṭȧ, *having run*.

B. The Negative forms are obtained by adding ആതെ āte, and ആഞ്ഞു് āññȧ, to the Conjugational base of the present (or future) tenses of verbs. The former is of indefinite tense and the latter of the past tense, e.g.

കളിക്കാതെ, *without playing, without having played.*
kaḷikkāte.

കളിക്കാഞ്ഞു്, *without*, or *through not having played.*
kaḷikkāññȧ.

The first form is often strengthened by the addition of the increment കണ്ടു് kaṇṭȧ, the past adverbial participle of the verb കാൺ kāṇ, *to see*. The second takes ഇട്ടു് iṭṭȧ ; e.g.

കളിക്കാതെകണ്ടു്, *without playing*, etc.
kaḷikkātēkaṇṭȧ.

കളിക്കാഞ്ഞിട്ടു്, *without* or *through not having played.*
kaḷikkāññiṭṭȧ.

C. These participles require a finite verb to complete the sentence ; e.g.

അവൻ ഓടി വന്നു് പറഞ്ഞു
avan ōṭi vannȧ paraññu.
He came running and said (lit. *he having run, having come, said.*

Thus, in translating into Malayāḷam, whenever a subject has two or more verbs, it is best to translate all but the last of them by the participle. The Malayāḷam language recognises only one finite verb in a sentence, simple or compound.

VERBAL AND ABSTRACT NOUNS.

Participial Nouns. By the addition of the personal terminations of the third person an, aḷ, tu for the singular, ar, va (a) for the plural to the present, past and negative relative participles, a large number of participial nouns are formed ; thus from the participles തിന്നുന്ന tinnunna, തിന്ന tinna, തിന്നാത്ത tinnātta, തിന്നാഞ്ഞ tinnāñña, of the verb തിൻ tin, *to eat*, are obtained :—

തിന്നുന്നവൻ, *he who eats* തിന്നവൾ, *she who ate.*
tinnunnavan tinnavaḷ.

തിന്നതു്, *that which ate*, or *that which was eaten,*
tinnatȧ.

തിന്നാത്തവർ, *they who do (did* or *will) not eat.*

തിന്നാഞ്ഞവർ, *they who did not eat.*

All these participial nouns usually take a subject, and have the same governing power as the verbs from which they are derived. They are, moreover, declined as any noun ; e.g.

കുററം ചെയ്തവനെ രാജാവു ശിക്ഷിച്ചു
kuṟṟam ceytavane rājāvȧ śikṣiccu.
The king punished the doer of (lit. *him who did*) *the crime.*

Another class of verbal nouns, meaning the act or action of the verb, is formed by adding ഉക uka (often shortened to ക ka, or അ a) to the conjugational base of the present (or future) tense of verbs. These are practically replaceable by the neuter noun formed from the present relative participle, e.g.

നുണ പറയുക (പറക) (*or* പറയുന്നതു്) നന്നല്ല
nuṇa paṟayuka (paṟaka) (paṟayunnatȧ) ṅannalla.
Speaking lies is not good.

അൽ al (sometimes ച്ചിൽ ccil, ക്കൽ kkal, ത്തൽ ttal, etc.) is added to some verbs to give a similar verbal noun with governing power ; e.g.

കുട്ട മെടയൽ, *The weaving of baskets.*
kuṭṭa meṭayal.

കുറച്ചിൽ, *lessening (disgrace).*
kuṟaccil.

തടുക്കൽ, *obstructing.*
taṭukkal.

നാടു കടത്തൽ, *deportation.*
nāṭu kaṭattal.

Verbal nouns expressing only the abstract idea, and with no governing power, are formed by the conversion of verbal roots into nouns, with or without modification, and the addition of such terminations as ma, am, vi, va, ȧ, vȧ, etc., e.g. നേർമ്മ nērmma, *lightness*, from നേർ nēr, *to become thin* or *light ;* കൂട്ടം kūṭṭam, *a conglomeration*, from കൂട്ടു് kūṭṭȧ ; മറവി maṟavi, *forgetfulness ;* കറവ kaṟava, *milking*, from കറ kaṟa ; പാട്ടു് pāṭṭȧ, *song*, from പാടു് pāṭȧ ; മറവു് maṟavȧ, *a covering, a mole*, from മറ maṟa ; ചുരുൾ curuḷ, *a roll*, from ചുരുൾ curul; ചുരുട്ടു് curuṭṭȧ, a *roll, a cigar*, from ചുരുട്ടു് curuṭṭȧ, etc. (See Derivative Cognate and allied nouns in the table, of verbs, pp. 84-113).

Infinitive Mood.

The true Dravidian Infinitive (corresponding to குளிக்க *to bathe*, வர *to come*, etc., in Tamil) is formed by adding അ a to the Conjugational base of the present (or future) tense.

This form, however, survives in Malayāḷam only* in combination with the auxiliary verb വേൺ vēn, *to be necessary.*

The Infinitive in common use is the infinitive of purpose which is formed by the addition of the termination ഉവാൻ uvān (shortened to ആൻ ān) to the Conjugational base of the present or future tense. Strong verbs have an additional form obtained by adding പ്പാൻ (ppān) to the root ; e.g.

നടക്കുവാൻ naṭakkuvān നടക്കാൻ naṭakkān നടപ്പാൻ naṭappān	*to walk*	പറയുവാൻ paṟayuvān പറയാൻ paṟayān പറവാൻ paṟavān	*to say.*

വേണ്ടി vēṇṭi, the past adverbial participle of വേൺ vēṇ, and ആയിട്ടു āyiṭṭả, those of ആകു ākả, and ഇടു iṭả, are used as strengthening increments to the infinitive of purpose. Thus :—

അയപ്പാൻ വേണ്ടി, *in order to send.*
ayappān vēṇṭi.

പോകുവാനായിട്ടു, *in order to go.*
pōkuvān āyiṭṭa.

Imperative Mood.

Either the crude base of a Malayāḷam verb, or the form obtained by adding ് ả to the conjugational base of its present (or future tense) is its second person singular imperative ; as നട naṭa, or നടക്കു naṭakkả, *walk (thou).*

---

* A fact which has led to its being confused with the verbal noun in ഉക. *Should do* is ചെയ്യ വേണം=ചെയ്യേണം and not ചെയ്യു വേണം, though the latter gives the same meaning.

The plural is formed by the addition of ഉവിൻ uvin (contracted to ഇൻ in) to the conjugational base of the present tense. In the case of strong verbs an alternative form is obtained by adding പ്പിൻ ppin. Thus :—

നടക്കുവിൻ
naṭakkuvin
നടക്കിൻ
naṭakkin
നടപ്പിൻ
naṭappin
} *walk*

പറയുവിൻ
paṟayuvin
പറയിൻ
paṟayin
പറവിൻ
paṟavin
} *say*

Intermediate forms, indicating neither respect nor lack of respect are (1) the verbal noun in ഉക **uka (see page 121)** and (2) the form obtained by adding ഉ u to the conjugational base of the present tense ; as

നടക്കുക
naṭakkuka
നടക്കു
naṭakku
} *walk*

The negative imperative or ' prohibitive is obtained by adding അരുതു arutŭ the obsolete past of the defective verb അരു aru to the conjugational base of the present tense ; as

അടിക്കരുതു aṭikkarutŭ, *do not beat.*

With the addition of the participle of emphasis, ഏ ē, the prohibition becomes a request ; as
അടിക്കരുതേ aṭikkarutē (*please*) *do not beat.*

Potential, Optative and Desiderative Forms.

A verbal form answering to the English potential mood is obtained by the addition of കഴിയും kaṟiyum to the infinitive of purpose ; the subject of this has to be put in the dative case.

എനിക്കു് അതു് ചെയ്യാൻ കഴിയും, *I can do it* (lit. *to me, it*
enikkȧ atȧ ceyyān kaṛiyum *to do is possible.*

ആം, no doubt a contraction of ആകും ākum, the future of ആകു് ākȧ, *to become, to be able,* added to the true Dravidian infinitive gives another form, implying here the idea of permission. The subject is usually to be put in the dative case, except in certain cases when it is in the Nominative. Thus :—

നിനക്കു പോകാം, *you may go* (*I give you permission to go*).
ninakku pōkām.

അവൻ പോകാം എന്നു് പറയുന്നു, *he says that he would go*
avan pōkām ennȧ paṛayunnu (*that he is willing to go*).

Optative and Desiderative expressions can be formed by (i.) the termination അട്ടെ aṭṭe, added to the conjugational base of the present tense ; as

ഞാൻ പോകട്ടെ, *let me go.*
ñān pōkaṭṭe

അവൻ ഓടട്ടെ, *let him run.*
avan ōṭaṭṭe.

(ii.) the conjugated forms of the defective verb വേൺ vēṇ (contracted to ഏൺ ēṇ) added to the true Dravidian infinitive.

അവൻ പോകേണം, *he must* or *should go.*
avan pōkēṇam

നീ പഠിക്കേണം, *you should study.*
nī paṭikkēṇam.

Permission is often expressed by the imperative of the auxiliary verb കൊള്ളു് koḷ (contracted to ഓൾ ōḷ), added to the past adverbial participle of verbs, as

എടുത്തു ' കൊള്ളു eṭuttu-koḷḷu, *you may take.*
(എടുത്തോളു) (= eṭuttōḷu).

Verbal Forms signifying Condition and Concession.

There are three ways of obtaining a Subjunctive or Conditional form. The first is by adding ആൽ āl to the past adverbial participle, and is of indefinite tense; as,

നീ അതു ചെയ്താൽ, *if you do (did,* or *will do) it.*
nī atȧ ceytāl.

The second way is to add എങ്കിൽ eṅkil (the subjunctive of the defective verb എൻ en) to the various tense forms, affirmative and negative. Thus:—

നീ അതു ചെയ്യുന്നെങ്കിൽ, *if you do it* (or *are doing it*).
nī atȧ ceyyunneṇkil.

നീ അതു ചെയ്തെങ്കിൽ, *if you did it* (or *have done it*).
nī atȧ ceyteṅkil.

നീ അതു ചെയ്യുമെങ്കിൽ, *if you will do it.*
nī atȧ ceyyumeṅkil

നീ അതു ചെയ്യുന്നില്ലെങ്കിൽ, *if you do not* (or *will not*) *do it.*
nī atȧ ceyyunnilleṅkil.

നീ അതു ചെയ്തില്ലെങ്കിൽ, *if you did not do it.*
nī atȧ ceytilleṅkil.

നീ അതു ചെയ്യുകയില്ലെങ്കിൽ. *if you will not do it*.*
nī atȧ ceyyukayilleṅkil.

A third method is to add ആകുന്നു ākunnu (contracted to ആണു āṇȧ), അല്ല alla, ഇല്ല illa to the verbal nouns in ഉക uka, and then to super-impose eṅkil; as

* See negative verbs page 114.

നീ അതു ചെയ്കയാണെങ്കിൽ, *if you are* (or *will be*) *doing it; if*
nī atȧ ceykayāṇeṅkil. *you were to do it.*

നീ അതു ചെയ്കയല്ലെങ്കിൽ, *if you are not doing it.*
nī atȧ ceykayalleṅkil.

നീ അതു ചെയ്കയില്ലെങ്കിൽ, *if you will not do it.*
nī atȧ ceykayilleṅkil.

എന്നാൽ ennāl, a subjunctive of the defective verb എൻ en is often used to express a reason (it is also sometimes used in place of എങ്കിൽ eṅkil).

e.g.

സൂത്രം ഫലിച്ചു; എങ്ങിനെ എന്നാൽ, ശത്രുക്കൾ ഭയപ്പെട്ടു മടങ്ങി, *The trick succeeded,* because, *the enemy retreated, frightened.*
sūtram paliccu; eṅṅine ennāl, śatrukka bayappeṭṭȧ maṭaṅṅi.

By the addition of ഉം um, to the subjunctive, or to the past adverbial participle of a verb, strengthened by ഇട്ടു iṭṭȧ (see page (A) above), an adverbial clause of concession, with indefinite tense, can be formed

പശു ചത്താലും, *even though the cow be dead.*
paśu cattālum

പറഞ്ഞിട്ടും ഫലമില്ല, *even after saying, there is no use.*
paṟaññiṭṭum palamilla.

Auxiliary and Defective Verbs.

The following are some of the commonest auxiliary verbs*—

ആക് ākȧ, *to be, to remain.*

വെയ് vey, *to place.*

ഇട് iṭȧ, ഈട് īṭȧ, *to put.*

കള kaḷa, *to lose*

കൊടു koṭu, *to give (him, her, them it.)*

തരു tarȧ, *to give (me, you)*

തീരു tīrȧ, *to end in.*

കഴി kaṛi, *to end in, to be able to.*

പോകു pōkȧ, *to go.*

വരു varȧ, *to come.*

കൂടു kūṭȧ, *to join.*

കൊൾ koḷ, *to affect.*

ഇരി iri, *to sit, remain.*

These are added to the മുൻവിനയെച്ചം munvinayeccam (the past adverbial participle), the പിൻ വിനയെച്ചം (the future adverbial participle), and the നടുവിനയെച്ചം (the true Dravidian Infinitive*) of verbs (A) to modify the meaning of the verbs or (B) to indicate time. (See page 81).

A. Appended are a few sentences illustrative of the uses of the more important auxiliaries in the above list.

കൊള്ളു   അതു കട്ടുംകൊണ്ടു കള്ളന്മാർ ഓടിക്കളഞ്ഞു
koḷ   atȧ kaṭṭumkoṇṭȧ kaḷḷanmār ōṭikkalaññu
Having stolen it, the thieves ran away.

അതു എടുത്തുകൊള്ളു (എടുത്തോളു)
atȧ eṭuttukoḷḷu (eṭuttōḷu), *You may take it.*

കള   കള്ളന്മാർ ഓടിക്കളഞ്ഞു
kaḷa   kaḷḷanmār ōtikkaḷaññu.
The thieves ran away.

---

* i.e. the infinitive in അ a, ക്ക kka as in വര vara *to come,* തടുക്ക taṭukka, *to obstruct.*

പോ അവൻ സ്വകാര്യം പറഞ്ഞുപോയി

pō avan svakāryam paṟaññå pōyi.

He has let out the secret (could not help it).

വരു് ശ്രമം മുറക്കു് നടന്നു് വരുന്നു

varå śṟamam muṟakkå naṭannå varunnu.

The endeavour continues with the usual persistence.

B. ഇരി iri, *to remain*, ആകു് ākå, *to become*, ഉള് uḷ, *to exist*, ഇടു് iṭå, *to put*, are important auxiliary or defective verbs which are used to form the compound tenses. Thus :—

ഞാൻ അതു് ചെയ്തിരിക്കുന്നു, *I have done it.*

ñān atå ceyt'-irikkunnu

ഞാൻ അതു് ചെയ്തിട്ടുണ്ടു്; *I have done it.*

ñān atå ceyt'-iṭṭ'-uṇṭå.

ഞാൻ അതു് ചെയ്തിരുന്നു, *I had done* (or *had been*) *doing it.*

ñān atå ceyt'-irunnu

അവൻ അതു് ചെയ്തിരിക്കും, *He would have done it.*

avan atå ceyt'-irikkum

അവൻ അതു് ചെയ്തിരിക്കാം, *He may have done it.*

avan atå ceyt'-irikkām

ഞാൻ അതു് ചെയ്തിട്ടുണ്ടായിരുന്നു, *I had done it.*

ñān atå ceyt'-iṭṭ'-uṇṭ'-ay'-irunnu.

അവൻ അതു് ചെയ്തിട്ടുണ്ടായിരിക്കും, *He would have done it.*

avan atå ceyt'-iṭṭ'-uṇṭ'-ay'-irikkum

അവൻ അതു് ചെയ്യുന്നുണ്ടു്, *He is doing it.*

avan atå ceyyunn'-uṇṭå

അവൻ അതു് ചെയ്കയായിരുന്നു, *He was doing it.*

avan atå ceyka-y-āy'-irunnu

അവൻ അതു് ചെയ്യുമായിരിക്കും, *He might do it.*

avan atå ceyyum-āy'-irikkum

അവൻ അതു് ചെയ്യുമായിരുന്നു, *He might have done it.*

avan atå ceyyum-āy'-irunnu' etc,

Defective Verbs.

Most of these are used as auxiliaries. Below is a list of the more important with their existent parts.

ഉൾ Past ഉണ്ടു് used in the sense of the present *there is*.
ul unṭå

Future ഉള്ളൂ = *there is* (only).
ullu

Pres. Adj. Part. ഉള്ള = *which exists.*
ulla

എൻ Past Adv. Part. എന്നു, *that* in *he said that he was coming.*
en ennå

Past Adj. Part. എന്ന = *who, or which is.*
enna

അൽ Future അല്ല = (*It is*) *not.*
al alla

ഇൽ ,, ഇല്ല = (*there is*) *not.*
il illa

ഒൽ Future ഒല്ല = *do not* (Imperative).
ol olla

അരു Past അരുതു് = *do not* (Imperative).
aru arutå

വേൺ Future വേണം = *must, is wanted* or *necessary.*
vēṇ vēṇam

Pres. Adj Part. വേണ്ടുന്ന = *which is necessary.*
vēṇṭunna

Past Adj. Part. വേണ്ടിയ = *which is* or *was necessary.*
vēṇṭiya

Future Adj. Part. വേണ്ടും = *which is necessary.*
vēṇṭum

തകു് Past Adj. Part. തക്ക = *which is fit or suitable.*
takå takka

മികു് mikå — Past Adj. Part. മിക്ക mikka = *most* as in *most people, most things.*

Passive Voice.

The Passive form, of which actual use is seldom made, is formed by the addition of the auxiliary പെടു peṭu, in all its inflections to the നടുവിനയെച്ചം naṭuvinayeccam (or infinitive in അ, ആ) e.g.

കള്ളൻ പിടിക്കപ്പെട്ടു, *The thief was caught.*
kaḷḷan piṭikka-p-peṭṭu

ADVERBS.

(*a*) A number of past adverbial participles serve as adverbs e.g. ഒരുമിച്ചു് orumiccå, *together.*

(*b*) As a rule, however, adverbs are formed from substantives by the addition of ആയി, or ആയ് āyi or āy; e.g. നല്ലതു് nallatå, *a good thing;* നല്ലതായ് nallatāy, *well;* തക്കതു് takkatå, *a suitable thing;* തക്കതായ് takkatāy, *suitably.*

(*c*) Some substantives are used directly as adverbs; e.g. വേഗം vēgam, *speed* for *quickly;* നിശ്ചയം niscayam, *certainty* for *certainly.*

POSTPOSITIONS.

Most of these are really parts of verbs, used as particles. Several are formed by adding ഏ e to the true Dravidian infinitive; e.g. ഒഴികെ oṛike, *except.* These govern the nouns they follow.

Similarly, പോലെ pōle, *like,* പററി paṟṟi, *about* govern the accusative. But അടുത്തു് aṭuttå, *near,* governs the genitive or dative, e.g. അതിൻെറ അടുത്തു atinre atuttȧ or അതിന്നടുത്തു atinnatuttȧ, *near it.* Similarly, കൂടെ kuṭe, *together*, governs the genitive or the instrumental; as, അവരുടെ കൂടെ avaruṭe kūṭe, or അവരോടു കൂടെ avarōṭȧ kūṭe, *together with them.*

Other post-positions in common use are :—

കൊണ്ടു koṇṭȧ, *by means of, about, because of.*

കുറിച്ചു kuṟiccȧ, *about.*

ഉള്ളിൽ uḷḷil, *within.*

പുറത്തു puṟattȧ, *outside.*

മുമ്പു mumpȧ, *before.*

പിമ്പു pimpȧ, *after.*

മുതൽ mutal, *beginning from.*

വഴി vaṟi, *by means of*

കീഴെ kiṟe, *below.*

വരെ vare, *up to, as long as.*

വരെക്കും varaykkum, *until.*

കൂടാതെ kūṭāte, *without.*

CONJUNCTIONS.

ഉം um added to two or more co-ordinate words means, *and.* When affixed to a single word it has the signification of *also, even* or *too*, according to the context.

ആനയും കുതിരയും കാലാളുകളും, *The elephants, the horses*
ānayum, kutiṟayum kālāḷukaḷum. *and the infantry.*

അവനും പോയി, *Even he, went.*
avanum pōyi.

Um is also used to express universality; as, എവിടെ eviṭe, *where,* എവിടെയും eviṭeyum, *everywhere.*

(*b*) *Or* = അല്ലെങ്കിൽ allenkil. The Correlatives *either..or* are obtained by adding ഓ ō to the different words in the same manner as ഉം um ; as അവരോ ഇവരോ, avarō, ivarō, *those or these.*

INTERROGATIVES.

To ask a question, you simply add ഓ ō to the end of a sentence or any word in it on which you wish to lay a stress; e.g.,

അവൻ തോട്ടക്കാരനാണൊ, *Is he a gardener?*
avan tōttakkāranāṇō.

The verb is sometimes displaced to before the subject or to before the extension of the predicate, as:—

അവൻ ചെയ്തുവോ അങ്ങിനെ ? *Did he do like that?*
avan ceytuvō aṅṅine ?
അങ്ങിനെ ചെയ്തുവൊ അവൻ ? *Did he do like that?*
aṅṅine ceytuvō avan ?

(*b*) Interrogative words are usually put first, and the impersonal verb ആകു ākụ, *to be*, is used with the neuter participial noun of the main verb. Thus—

എവിടെക്കു ആണു* പൊകുന്നതു? *Where is it that (you) are going?*
evitekkụ āṇā pōkunnatụ ?

is a more usual construction than

എവിടെക്കു പോണു*, *Where do you go?*
eviṭekku pōṇu.

---

*ആണു āṇạ and പോണു pōṇu are colloquial abbreviations of ആകുന്നു ākunnu and പോകുന്നു pōkunnu.

EMPHATIC PARTICLES.

The vowel ഏ ē is added to words for the sake of emphasis ; as,

കഷ്ടമേ ഉണ്ടാകൂ, *There will only be trouble.*
kaṣtamē uṇṭāku.

The reflexive pronoun തന്നെ is also used to emphasis nouns, when it serves as the predicate ; as

അവൻ മിടുക്കൻ തന്നെ, *He is indeed a clever man.*
avan miṭukkan tanne.

Also അല്ലോ allō is used to make statements of general acceptability :—

ആന ഒരു വലിയ മൃഗമാണല്ലോ, *The elephant is a big*
āna oru valiya mṛgamāṇallo. *animal, is it not ?*

INTERJECTIONS.

The following are some of them :—

അയ്യോ ayyo, *alas !*
അയ്യയ്യോ ayyayyo, *alas ! alas !*
അതാ atā, *there it is !*
ഇതാ itā, *lo !*
ഓ ഹോ ō hō ! *Oh !*

CONVERSATIONAL PHRASES.

Useful and Necessary Idiomatic Expressions and Phrases.

Upayōgavum Āvaśyavum uḷḷatum Bāṣāśailikkottatum āya Vākya-pṟayōgaṅṅal.

English.	Malayalam.	Pronunciation.
Thank you (to servants)	koḷḷām	ko*llah*m
(to equals and superiors)	ñān nandi paṟayunnu	*nyah*n n'un'n'i puṟayo͞on'n'o͞o
Have the goodness to do such and such a thing	dayavu ceytả, inna kāryam ceytāl koḷḷām	*th*ayuwŭ cheyth'ŭ, innu k*ah*ryam cheyth'*ah*l ko*llah*m
Yes (there is)	uvvả	o͞owwŭ
Yes (it is so)	ate	uth'e
Bring me	koṇṭu varu (or varika)	ko*n*t'ŭ wuro͞o (*or* wurik'u)
,, (to servants)	koṇṭu vā	ko*n*t'ŭ w*ah*
,, (respectfully)	koṇṭu vannāl koḷḷām	ko*n*t'ŭ wun'n'*ah*l ko*llah*m
Give me	enikku taru (or tarika)	enikkŭ thuro͞o (*or* thurik'ŭ)
,, (respectfully)	enikku tannāl koḷḷām	enikkŭ thun'n'*ah*l ko*llah*m
Send it to me	atả enikku ayakku (*or* ayakkuka)	uth'ŭ enikkŭ uyakko͞o (*or* uyakko͞ok'u)
,, (respectfully)	atả enikku ayaccāl koḷḷām	uth'ŭ enikkŭ uyachch*ah*l ko*llah*m

English.	Malayalam.	Pronunciation.
Send it to him	atȧ addēhattinnȧ ayakku (or ayakkuka)	uth'ŭ u*hthay*huththinnŭ uyakko͝o (*or* uyakko͝ok'u)
„ (respectfully)	atȧ addēhattinnȧ ayaccāl koḷḷām	uth'ŭ u*hthay*huththinnŭ uyachch*ahl* ko*llah*m
Tell me	ennōṭu paṟayu	enn*oh*t'ŭ puṟayo͝o
Will you tell me ?	niṅṅaḷ ennōṭu paṟayumō ?	n'iṉgṉgu*l* enn*oh*t'ŭ puṟayo͝om*oh*
Do you understand?	manassil ākunnuṇṭō ?	munassil *ah*k'o͝on' n'o͝o*n*t'*oh*
Excuse me	enikku māppu tarika	enikkŭ m*ah*ppŭ thurik'u
Do you speak English ?	niṅṅaḷkku iṅkḷīṣu samsārippān aṟiyumō ?	n'iṉgṉgu*l*kkŭ iṉgk'*l*eeshŭ sums*ah*rip*pah*n uṟiyo͝om*oh*
Does anyone here speak English ?	iviṭe āṟkkeṅkilum iṅkḷīṣu samsārippān aṟiyumō ?	iwit'e *ah*ṟkkeṉgk'ilo͝om iṉgk'leeshŭ sums*ah*ripp*ah*n uṟiyo͝om*oh*
Can you read English ?	niṅṅaḷkku iṅkḷīṣu vāyippān kaṟiyumō ?	n'iṉgṉgu*l*kkŭ iṉgk'*l*eeshŭ w*ah*yipp*ah*n kuṟiyo͝om*oh*
Have patience	kuraccu kṣamikkuka	ko͝oṟachchŭ k'shumikko͝ok'u
What do you say ?	niṅṅaḷ entāṇȧ paṟayunnatȧ ?	n'iṉgṉgu*l* en'th'*ah*nŭ puṟayo͝on'n'uth'ŭ
I beg your pardon	māppu, ñān kēṭṭilla	m*ah*ppŭ, *nyah*n k*ay*ttillu
What did you ask (question) ?	niṅṅaḷ entāṇȧ cōdiccatȧ ?	n'iṉgṉgu*l* en'th'*ah*nŭ ch'*ohth*ichchath'ŭ?
What did you ask (request) ?	niṅṅaḷ entāṇȧ āvaśya-p-peṭṭatȧ ?	n'iṉgṉgu*l* en'th'*ah*nŭ *ah*wasyu-p-pettuth'ŭ
Speak louder	uṟakke paṟayuka	o͝oṟukke puṟayo͝ok'u
What does it signify ?	atinṟe aṟttam entȧ?	uth'inṯe uṟththum en'th'ŭ

English.	Malayalam.	Pronunciation.
It doesn't matter	atȧ sāram illa	uth'ŭ s*ah*rum illu
It is all the same to me	enikkatil ētu vidam āyālum śari	enikkuth'il *ay*th'ŭ wi*th*um *ahyah*lōōm suri
Never mind	atȧ sāram illa	uth'ŭ s*ah*rum illu
What is to be done ?	entāṇu ceyyēṇṭatȧ?	en'th'*ahn*ŭ ch'ey-*ayn*t'uth'ŭ
Do you hear ?	kēḷkkunnō ? (or kiṭṭō ?)	k*ayl*kkōōn'n'*oh* ? (*or* kitt*oh*)
I understand	enikku manassil-āyi	enikkŭ munassil-*ah*yi
I don't understand	enikku manassil-ā-kunnilla	enikku mŭnassil-*ah*-kōōn'n'illu
Carry this	itȧ eṭuttu-koṇṭu-varika	ithŭ et'ōōththŭk*on*-t'ŭ-wurik'u
Take this	itȧ eṭukkuka	ith'ŭ et'ōōkkōōk'u
Take this away	itȧ eṭuttu-koṇṭu-pōka	ith'ŭ et'ōōththŭ-k*on*-t'ŭ-p*oh*k'u
Why are you so slow ?	niṅṅalkku entāṇȧ itṟa sāvadānam ?	n'ingngu*l*kkŭ en'th'-*ahn*ŭ ithṟu s*ah*wu-*thah*nam
Make haste !	dṟti vekku	*thr*th'i wekkōō
Come along !	pōka, varin	p*oh*k'u, wurin
Take care !	sūkṣikka	sook'shikku
Look out	śṟadda vekkuka	sṟa*th*thu wekkōōk'u
Listen (to this)	itȧ kēkku	ith'ŭ k*ay*kkōō
Come in	akattēkku varu	ukuthth*ay*kkŭ wurōō
Come here	iviṭe varu	iwit'e wurōō
Come back	tiriccu varu	thirichchŭ wurōō
Call my servant	enṟe vālikkāranc vi-ḷikkuka	enṭe w*ah*likk*ah*rane wi*l*ikkōōk'u
Take this note	ī eṟuttȧ eṭukkuka	ee eṟōōththŭ et'ōōk-kōōk'u
Bring an answer	maṟuvati koṇṭu va-rika	muṟōōwut'i k*on*t'ŭ-wurik'u
Stand still	anaṅṅātc nilkkuka	unangng*ah*th'e n'ik-kōōk'u

English.	Malayalam.	Pronunciation.
Go away	puṟattu pōka	pooṟaththŭ pohk'u
That way	ā vaṟiye	*ah* wuṟiye
This way	ī vaṟiye	ee wuṟiye
Too soon	vallāte vēgam	wull*ah*th'e w*ay*gam
Too late	vallāte vaiki	wull*ah*th'e w*i*k'i
What do you want ?	niṅṅaḷkku entá vēṇam ?	n'ingngu*l*kkŭ en'th'ŭ w*ay*n*um*
Will you do me a favour ?	niṅṅaḷ enikku oru upakāram ceyyāmō ?	n'ingngu*l* enikkŭ o-roo oopuk'*ah*ram cheyy*ah*m*oh*
What is it ?	entāṇá atá ?	en'th'*ah*nŭ uth'ŭ
I am (or shall be) very much obliged to you	ñān niṅṅaḷōṭu vaḷare nandi uḷḷavan āyirikkunnu (āyirikkum)	*nyah*n n'ingngu*loh*t'ŭ wu*l*ure n'un'n'i oo*l**l*awun *ah*yirikkoon'n'oo (*ah*yirikkoom)
Very well	vaḷare nallatá	wu*l*ure n'ulluth'ŭ
I am sorry to trouble you so much	niṅṅaḷe iṅṅine upadravikkunnatil vyasanikkunnu	n'ingngu*l*e ingngine oop'u*th*ruwik-koon n'uth'il wyasunikkoon'n'oo
No trouble at all	upadravam oṭṭum illa	oop'u*th*ruwum ottoom illu
What is the matter with you (your health) ?	niṅṅalkku entā sukakkēṭu ?	n'ingngu*l*kkŭ en'-th'*ah* sookukk*ay*-t'ŭ
What is the matter with (troubling) you ?	niṅṅaḷuṭe manassil entā kāryam uḷḷatá ?	n'ingngu*l*oot'e mu-nassil en'th'*ah* k*ah*ryam oo*ll*uthŭ
What is the matter?	entā samgati ?	en'th'*ah* sungnguth'i
Nothing	onnum illa	on'n'oom illu
Who is there ?	ārāṇá aviṭe ?	*ah*r*ah*nŭ uwit'e
It is I	atá ñān tanne	uth'ŭ *nyah*n thunne
What is the news ?	entā vaṟtamānam	en'th'*ah* wuṟthum*ah*-num
Have you any news?	valla vaṟtamānavum uṇṭō ?	wullu wuṟthum*ah*nu-woom oo*n*t'*oh*

English.	Malayalam.	Pronunciation.
I have heard nothing	ñān onnum kēṭṭiṭṭilla	*nyah*n on'n'o͞om k*ay*ttittillu
Are you quite certain ?	niṅṅaḷkku nalla tīṟcca uṇṭō ?	n'ingngu*l*kkŭ n'ullu theeṟchchu o͞o*n*-t'*oh*
What has happened	entāṇȧ uṇṭāyatȧ ? (or entāṇȧ sambaviccatȧ ?)	en'th'*ahn*ŭ o͞o*n*t'*ah*-yath'ŭ (*or* en'-th*ahn*ŭ sumbu-wichchuth'ŭ
What temple is that ?	atȧ ētȧ ampalam āṇȧ ?	uth'ŭ *ay*th'ŭ ump'u-lum *ahn*ŭ
What church is that ?	atȧ ētȧ paḷḷi āṇȧ ?	uth'ŭ *ay*th'ŭ pu*ll*i *ahn*ŭ
Begone or Go	pō (or pōvu kaṭannȧ)	p*oh* (*or* p*oh*wo͞o ku-t'an'n'ŭ)
Go home	vīṭṭilekku pōvu	weettilekkŭ p*oh*wo͞o
Go to the post-office and bring my letters	tappāl-āppīssil pōyi enṟe eṟuttukaḷ vāṅṅi-k-koṇṭu varika	thupp*ah*l-*ah*ppeessil po*h*yi enṯe eṟo͞oth-tho͞oku*l* w*ah*ngngi-k-ko*n*t'ŭ wurik'u
Show me the house of the Consul	kōṇsaḷinṟe vīṭu kāṭ ṭi-t-tarika	k*ohn*su*l*inṯe weet'ŭ k*ah*tti-th-thurik'u
Let us start (set out)	namukku puṟappeṭām	n'umo͞okkŭ po͞oṟup-pet'*ah*m
„ (begin)	namukku tuṭaṅṅām	n'umo͞okkŭ tho͞o-t'angng*ah*m
Get everything ready	ellām tayyāṟ-ākki-vekkuka	ell*ah*m thayy*ah*ṟ-*ah*kki wekko͞ok'u
Wait (a little)	(alpam) tāmasikku	(ulpum) th*ah*musik-ith'*ah*
Here I am	itā ñān	*nyah*n [ko͞o
Be good enough to tell me	dayavu ceytȧ ennōṭȧ paṟaññālum	,*th*uyaw ŭ cheyth'ŭ en-n*oh*t'ŭ puṟ*any-nyah*lo͞om
Hear what I tell you	ñān paṟayunnatȧ śṟaddikku	*nyah*n puṟayo͞on'n'u-th'ŭ sṟu*thth*ikko͞o
Do as I tell you	ñān paṟayunnatȧ kēḷkku	*nyah*n purayo͞on'n'u-th'ŭ k*ay*kko͞o

English.	Malayalam.	Pronunciation.
Bring (me) my horse	enṟe kutiraye koṇṭu varu	enṯe kŏŏth'iruye kont'ŭ wurŏŏ
Speak with the interpreter	dvibāṣiyum-āyi samsārikkuka	thwibahshiyŏŏm-ahyi sumsahrikkŏŏk'u
Speak to him	ayāḷōṭȧ samsārikka	uyahloht'ŭ sumsahrikku
What does this mean ?	itinṟe aṟttam entāṇȧ ?	ith'inṯe uṟththum enth'ahnŭ

Expressions of Emotion (Vikāra Pṟakaṭanaṅṅaḷ)

English.	Malayalam.	Pronunciation.
What ?	entȧ ?	en'th'ŭ
Is it possible ?	aṅṅine varumō ?	uṉgṉgine wurŏŏmoh
Indeed !	vāstavum !	wahsthuwum
That is impossible	at'asādyam	uth'usahthyam
That cannot be	aṅṅine varilla	uṉgṉgine wurillu
You surprise me	niṅṅaḷ enne atiśaya-ppeṭuttunnu	niṉgṉgul enne uthisayuppet'ŏŏththŏŏn'n'ŏŏ
Don't touch	toṭarutȧ	thot'urŏŏth'ŭ
My fault	enṟe teṟṟȧ	enṯe theṯṯŭ
Oh ! it's nothing	ēy ! atȧ sāram illa	ayy uth'ŭ sahram illu
I am sorry for it	enikkȧ atil vyasanam uṇṭȧ	enikkŭ uth'il wyasunam ŏŏnt'ŭ
I am quite vexed about it	enikkȧ atinekkuriccu vallāte muṣiccil tōnnunnu	enikkŭ uth'inekkŏŏṟichchŭ wullahth'e mŏŏshichchil thohn'n'ŏŏn'n'ŏŏ
What a pity !	entȧ kaṣṭam !	en'th'ŭ kusht'am
It is a sad thing	atȧ oru saṅkaṭam āya kāryam tanne	uth'ŭ orŏŏ sungk'ut'um ahyu kahryam thunne
Bravo !	bēṣ ! bale !	bavsh bule
Well done	ceytatu nannāyi	cheyth'uthŭ n'un'n'ahy
How fortunate !	etṟa bāgyamāyi !	ethṟu bahgyamahyi

English.	Malayalam.	Pronunciation.
How beautiful	enṭȧ bamgi	en'th'u bungngi
All right !	āṭṭe, śari !	*ah*tte, sari
I am very glad	enikku vaḷare samtōṣam uṇṭȧ	ènikkŭ wu*l*are sun'th'*oh*shum o͞o*nt*'u
How shocking !	entȧ katinam	en'th'ŭ kutinam
He is very angry	avan vallāte dēṣyappeṭṭirikkunnu	uwun wull*ah*th'e *thay*shyuppettirikko͞on'n'o͞o
What a shame !	entȧ kuṟavȧ ! entȧ pōrāyma !	en'th'ŭ ko͞oṟuwŭ, en'thŭ p*oh*r*ah*ymu
Serve you right	assal āyi	ussal *ah*yi
For shame	cī, cī	chee, chee
Hold your tongue	nākkȧ vayil kiṭakkaṭṭe	n*ah*kkŭ w*ah*yil ki t'akkutte
You are very much to blame	niṅṅaḷ vallātta teṟṟukāran	ningngu*l* wull*ah*ththu thettо͞ok*ah*ran
You ought to be ashamed of yourself	nāṇam illallō ?	n'*ahn*am illall*oh*

Notices (Parasyaṅṅaḷ)

Apartments (which are) to be let	vāṭakakku koṭuppān (uḷḷa) muṟikaḷ	w*ah*t'ak'ukkŭ kot'o͞opp*ah*n (o͞o*ll*u) mo͞oṟik'u*l*
Entrance	pravēśanam	pruw*ay*sanum
Exit	puṟattu pōkum vaṟi	po͞oṟuththŭ p*oh*k'o͞om wuṟi
Fire Alarm	tī-bāda aṟiyikkum yantram	thee-b*ahth*u uṟiyikko͞om yan'thrum
Furnished rooms	vīṭṭu-sāmānaṅṅaḷ uḷḷa muṟikal	weettŭ s*ah*m*ah*nungngu*l* o͞o*ll*u mo͞oṟik'u*l*
Knock ; ring	muṭṭuka ; maṇi-y-aṭikkuka	mo͞otto͞ok'u ; mu*n*i-y-ut'ikko͞ok'u
No admittance	pravēśanam illa	pruw*ay*sunum illu
No smoking	puka valikkarutȧ	po͞oku wulikkuro͞oth ŭ

English.	Malayalam.	Pronunciation.
No smoking allowed	puka valiccu kūṭa	poŏk'u wulichchŭ koot'u
No thoroughfare	itile vaṟi naṭakkaruta	ithile wuṟi n'ut'ukkurŏŏth'ŭ
Please do not touch	dayavu ceyta, toṭātirippin	*th*uyavŭ cheyth'ŭ, thot'*ah*th'irippin
Private	svakāryam	swuk'*ah*ryam
Public notice	parasyam ; aṟiyippu	purasyum ; uṟiyippŭ
Pull ; push	valikkuka ; taḷḷuka	wuḷikkŏŏk'u ; thu*l*-*l*ŏŏk'u
Refreshments	lagu bakṣaṇaṅṅaḷ	lagŏŏ buk'shu*n*uṉgṉgu*l*
To be let, to let	vāṭakakku koṭuppān	w*ah*t'ak'ukkŭ kot'ŏŏpp*ah*n
To be sold	vilpān	wilp*ah*n
Unfurnished rooms	sāmānaṅṅaḷ illātta muṟikaḷ	s*ah*m*ah*nuṉgṉgu*l* il*lah*ththu mŏŏṟik'u*l*
Walk in	akattu varika	uk'uththŭ wurik'u

The Railway (Tīvaṇṭi-p-pāta)

To the station	āppīssilekka	*ah*ppeessilekkŭ
Here is my luggage	enṟe sāmānam itā	enṭe s*ah*m*ah*num ith'*ah*
Take these to the cloak-room	ivaye sāmāna-s-sūkṣippu muṟiyilekku koṇṭu pōyi vekkuka	iwaye s*ah*m*ah*nu-s-sook'shippŭ mŏŏṟiyilekkŭ ko*n*t'ŭ po*h*yi wekkŏŏk'u
I wish to register my luggage to...	...kku enṟe sāmānam ṟajistṟākkēṇam ennuṇṭa	...kkŭ enṭe s*ah*m*ah*num ṟajisthṟ*ah*kk*ay*num en'n'ŏŏ*n*t'ŭ
The luggage is over weight	sāmānattinna adikat-tūkkam uṇṭa	s*ah*nuththinnŭ u*thi*ku-ththookkum ŏŏ*n*t'ŭ

English.	Malayalam.	Pronunciation.
Get my luggage ; here is the ticket	enṟe sāmānam eṭuttu-koṇṭu-varu ; śiṭṭu itā	enṯe s*ah*m*ah*num et'o͝oththŭ-ko*n*t'ŭ-wuro͝o ; seettŭ ith'*ah*
Where is the waiting-room	vaṇṭi kāttirikkum muṟi eviṭe āṇȧ ?	wu*n*t'i k*ah*ththirikko͝om muṟi ewit'e *ahn*ŭ
„ booking office	śiṭṭu vilkkum muṟi evite āṇȧ ?	seettŭ wikko͝om muṟi ewit'e *ahn*ŭ
Where is the buffet?	bakṣaṇa-stalam eviṭe ?	buk'shu*n*u-sthulam ewit'e
„ lavatory ?	kakkūs eviṭe ?	kukkoos ewit'e
Where is the train for...?	...kkuḷḷa vaṇṭi eviṭe āṇȧ ?	...kko͝o*ll*u wu*n*t'i ewit'e *ahn*ŭ
Are you going by the express	niṅṅaḷ vēga-vaṇṭiyil āṇō pōkunnatȧ ?	n'iṉgṉgu*l* w*ay*gu-wu*n*t'iyil *ahnoh* p*oh*ko͝on'n'uth'ŭ
Show me the time-table	enikku samaya-vivara-p-paṭṭika kāṇiccu tarika	enikkŭ sumayu-wiwuru-p-puttiku k*ahn*ichchŭ thurik'u
When does the train start ?	eppōṟāṇȧ vaṇṭi puṟap-peṭunnatȧ ?	epp*oh*ṟ*ahn*ŭ wu*n*t'i po͝oṟup-pet'o͝on'n'uth'ŭ
Can I book through to...?	...kku nēriṭṭu śiṭṭu vāṅṅān kaṟiyumō ?	...kkŭ n*ay*rittŭ seettŭ w*ah*ṉgṉg*ah*n kuṟiyo͝om*oh*
A first- (second-) class single ticket to...	...kku oru onnām-(raṇṭām) kḷāssu śiṭṭu...	...kkŭ oro͝o on'n'-*ah*m (ru*n*t'*ah*m) k*lah*ssŭ seettŭ...
Return tickets	maṭakka-ś-śiṭṭukaḷ	mut'ukku-s-seetto͝o-k'u*l*
How much is it ?	atinnȧ etṟa ?	uth'innŭ ethṟu
We want a sleeping carriage	ñaṅṅaḷkku oru uṟaṅṅān saukaryam uḷḷa vaṇṭi vēṇam	*ny*uṉgṉgu*l*kkŭ oro͝o o͝oṟuṉgṉg*ah*n s*ow*kuryam o͝o*ll*u wu*n*t'i w*ay*num

English.	Malayalam.	Pronunciation.
A corridor carriage	oru neṭu-vaṛi-y-uḷḷa vaṇṭi	oroo n'et'oo-wuṛi-yoo*ll*u wu*n*t'i
A carriage for ladies	oru stṛīkaḷ-k-kuḷḷa vaṇṭi	oroo sthṛeeku*l*koo*ll*u wu*n*t'i
A non-smoking compartment	oru puka valippān pāṭillātta vakuppa	oroo pook'u wulip-p*ah*n p*ah*till*ah*th-thu wuk'ooppŭ
Is this the train for ...?	itāṇō...kkuḷḷa vaṇṭi ?	ith*ahnoh*...ḳkoo*ll*u wu*n*t'i
Do I change anywhere on the journey ?	yātṛakku naṭuvil eviṭe-y-eṅkilum māṟi-k-kayaṟēṇamō ?	y*ah*thṛukkŭ n'ut'oowil ewit'e-y-eṉgk'iloom m*ah*ṛi-k-kuyaṛ*ay*numo*h* ?
Where must I change for...?	...kku eviṭe-y-āṇa māṟi-k-kayaṟēṇṭatā ?	...kkŭ ewit'e-y-*ahn*ŭ m*ah*ṛi-k-kuyaṛ*ahn*-t'uth'ŭ
Is this seat engaged ?	ī stalam āreṅkilum eṭuttiṭṭuṇṭō ?	ee sthulum *ah*reṉg-k'iloom et'ooth-thitto*o*n*t'*oh*
There is no room	stalam illa	sthulum illu
Call the guard	gārḍine viḷikkuka	g*ah*ṛdine wi*l*ikkook'u
The train is just going to start	vaṇṭi, itā ! puṟa-p-peṭān pōkunnu	wu*n*t'i, ith'*ah* poo-ru-p-pet'*ah*n p*oh*-k'oon'n'oo
Open the door	vātil tuṟakkuka	w*ah*th'il thooṛakkoo-k'u
Open the window	janēri tuṟakkuka	jun*ay*ri thooṛakkook'u
Here is the station	itā āppīssā	ith'*ah* *ah*ppeessŭ
Do we stop here ?	vaṇṭi iviṭe nilkkumō ?	wu*n*t'i iwit'e n'ikkoo-mo*h*
Do we alight here ?	nām iviṭe iṟaṅṅēṇamō ?	n'*ah*m iwit'e iṛuṉg-ṉg*ay*numo*h*
Do we change carriages here ?	nām iviṭe vaṇṭi māṟi-k-kayaṟēṇamō?	n'*ah*m iwit'e wu*n*t'i m*ah*ṛi-k-kuyaṛ*ay*-*numoh*
How long do we stop here ?	iviṭe etṛa nēram tāmasam uṇṭā ?	iwit'e ethṛu n'*ay*rum th*ah*musum oo*n*t'ŭ

English.	Malayalam.	Pronunciation.
Five minutes	añcu minuṭṭȧ	u*n*ych'ŭ minōōttŭ
My luggage is lost	enṟe sāmānam kāṇmānilla	enṯe s*ah*m*ah*num k*ahn*m*ah*nillu
When it arrives forward it on to ...	atȧ varumpōḷ ...... kku ayaccāl koḷḷām	uth'ŭ wurōōmp'*ohl* ... kkŭ uyachch*ahl* ko*ll**ah*m
Give me your ticket	niṅṅaḷuṭe śiṭṭu taru	n'iṉgṉgu*l*ōōt'e seettŭ thurōō
Here it is !	itā !	ith'*ah* !

The Hotel (Hōṭṭel).

Which is the best hotel ?	ellāttilum nalla hōṭṭel ētāṇȧ ?	ell*ah*ththilōōm n'ullu h*oh*ttel *ay*th'*ahn*ŭ?
Let us have supper soon	ñaṅṅaḷkku vēgam attāṟam tannālum	*ny*uṉgṉgu*l*kkŭ *way*gum uthth*ah*ṟum thun'n'*ah*lōōm
Are our rooms ready ?	ñaṅṅaḷuṭe muṟikaḷ tayyāṟ-uṇṭō ?	*ny*uṉgṉgu*l*ōōt'e mōōṟik'u*l* thayy*ah*ṟ-ōō*nt'oh*
I want a bed-room	enikku oru uṟakkaṟa vēṇam	enikkŭ orōō ōōṟukkuṟu w*ayn*um
Let me see the room	ñān muṟi kāṇaṭṭe	*nyah*n mōōṟi k*ahn*utte
What is the rent of this room ?	ī muṟikku vāṭaka entā ?	ee mōōṟikkŭ v*ah*t'uk'u en'th'*ah* [k'um
That is too dear	atȧ vaḷare adikam	uth'ŭ wu*l*ure u*th*i-
I want a cheaper room	ennikku itilum sahāyam āya oru muṟi vēṇam	enikkŭ ith'ilōōm su*hah*yam *ah*yu orōō mōōṟi w*ayn*um
Are there any letters for me ?	enikku valla eṟuttukaḷum uṇṭō ?	enikkŭ wullu eṟōōththōōk'**u*l*ōōm** ōō*n*t'*oh*
Where is the w.c. ?	kakkūs eviṭe ?	kukkoos ewit'e
Can I have a warm bath ?	enikku kuḷikkān cuṭu-veḷḷam tarumō ?	enikkŭ kōō*l*ikk*ah*n chōōt'ŭ-we*ll*um **thurōōm*oh***

English.	Malayalam.	Pronunciation.
Give me the key of my room	enṟe muṟiyuṭe tākkōl tarika	enṯe mŏŏṟiyŏŏt'e th*ah*kk*oh*l thurik'u
Bring me some warm water	kuraccu kāññā veḷḷam koṇṭu-vannā tarika	kŏŏṟachchŭ *kahny-nyu* we*ll*um ko*n*t'ŭ wun'n'ŭ thurik'u
Take my luggage down	enṟe sāmānam tāṟa-t-tekku eṭuttā-koṇṭu pōka	enṯe s*ah*m*ah*num th*ah*ṟuth-thekkŭ e-t'ŏŏththŭ-ḳ'o*n*t'ŭ p*oh*k'u
Give me a candle, please	enikku oru meṟutiri tannāl koḷḷām	enikkŭ orŏŏ meṟŏŏ-th'iri thun'n'*ah*l ko*ll*a*h*m
We leave early to-morrow morning	ñaṅṅal nāḷe rāvile nēṟtte pōkum	*ny*uṉgṉgu*l* n'*ah*l*e* r*ah*wile n*ay*ṟththe p*oh*k'ŏŏm
Call me at seven	enne ēṟu maṇikku viḷikkuka	enne *ay*ṟŭ mu*n*ikkŭ wi*l*ikkŏŏk'u
Wake me at five	enne añcu manikku uṇaṟttuka	enne u*ny*chŭ mu*n*ik-kŭ ŏŏ*n*aṟththŏŏk'u

Breakfast (Pṟātal)

English.	Malayalam.	Pronunciation.
Is breakfast ready ?	pṟātal tayyāṟ-āyō ?	pṟ*ah*th'al thuyy*ah*ṟ-*ah*y*oh*
Breakfast is ready	pṟātal tayyāṟ-āyi	pṟ*ah*th'al thuyy*ah*ṟ-*ah*yi
Is the tea made ?	cāya uṇṭākkiō ?	ch*ah*yu ŏŏ*nt*'*ah*kki-y*oh*
Do you drink...?	niṅṅaḷ ... kuṭikku-mō ?	n'iṉgṉgu*l* ... kŏŏt'ik-kŏŏm*oh*
This cream is sour	ī pāl-pāṭa puḷiccu pōyi	ee p*ah*l-p*ah*t'u pŏŏ-*l*ichchŭ p*oh*yi —
Will you take...?	niṅṅal ... kaṟikku-mō ?	n'iṉgṉgul ... kuṟik-kŏŏm*oh*
These eggs are hard	ī muṭṭakaḷ kallaccu pōyi	ee mŏŏttuk'u*l* kul-lachchŭ p*oh*yi

English.	Malayalam.	Pronunciation.
Give me some salt	kuṟaccu uppu taru	kōōṟachchŭ ōōppōō thurōō
Pass me the salt-cellar	uppu-kuppi iṅṅōṭṭu tarika	ōōppōō-k'ōōppi iṉg-ṉgohttŭ thurik'u
This butter is not fresh	ī veṇṇa pututā alla	ee vennu pōōth'ōō-th'ŭ ullu
Bring some more	kuṟaccu kūṭi koṇṭu varu	kōōṟachchŭ koot'i kont'ŭ-wurōō
Is the coffee strong enough ?	kāppikku vēṇṭa kaṭṭi uṇṭō ?	kahppikkŭ waynt'u kutti ōōnt'oh
We want more cups	kuṟe kōppakaḷ kūṭe vēṇam	kōōṟe kohppuk'ul koot'e waynum
Take some more...	... kuṟaccu kūṭi e-ṭukku	... kōōṟachchŭ koot'i et'ōōkkōō
A piece of toast	oru kaṣṇam ṭōsṟṟā (or poricca ṟoṭṭi)	orōō kushnum toh-sṭṭŭ (or porichchu ṟotti)
A rasher of bacon	oru kīṟā bēkkaṉ (or panni-māmsam)	orōō keeṟŭ baykkun (or pun'n'i-mahm-sum
Coffee with milk	kāppi	kahppi
Coffee without milk or cream	pacca-k-kāppi	puchchu-k-kahppi
Coffee only	kāppi mātṟam	kahppi mahthṟum
Remove these things (from the table)	(mēśamēl ninnā) ī sādanaṅṅaḷ nīk-kuka	maysumayl n'in'n'ŭ ee sahthanung-ngul n'eekkōōk'u

Dinner (Muttāṟam)

Show me the bill of fare	bakṣana-sādana-vivara paṭṭika kāṇiccu taru	buk'shunu - sahthu-nu-wiwuru puṭṭi-ku kahnichchŭ thurōō
What have you ready ?	entuṇṭā tayyāṟ-āyiṭṭā ?	en'th'ōōnt'ŭ thay-yahṟ-ahyittŭ
What soup will you have ?	niṅṅaḷ entu sūp-pā-ṇā kaṟikkunna-tā ?	n'iṉgṉgul en'th'ŭ soop-pahnŭ kuṟik-kōōn'n'ath'ŭ

English.	Malayalam.	Pronunciation.
May I give you some fish ?	kuraccu matsyam taraṭṭe ?	kōōṛachchŭ mulsyam thurutte
Fried seer-fish	poricca akilȧ	porichchu uk'ilŭ
What wine will you have ?	niṅṅalkku entu vīññu ānȧ vēṇṭatȧ ?	n'iṉgṉgu*l*kkŭ en'th'ŭ wee*nyny*ŭ *ahn*ŭ w*ayn*t'uth'ŭ
We shall dine at three o'clock	ñaṅṅaḷ mūnnu maṇikku ūṇ kaṛikkum	*ny*uṉgṉgu*l* moon'n'ŭ mu*n*ikkŭ oo*n* kuṛikkōōm
Are you hungry or thirsty ?	niṅṅaḷkku viśappō dāhamō uṇṭo ?	n'iṉgṉgu*l*kkŭ wisappo*h* *thah*humo*h* ōō*n*t'o*h*
I am very thirsty	enikku vallāte dāhikkunnu	enikkŭ wull*ah*th'e *thah*hikkōōn'n'ōō
What shall I help you to ?	niṅṅaḷkku ñān entāṇȧ eṭuttu-tarēṇṭatȧ ?	niṉgṉgu*l*kkŭ *nyah*n en'th'*ahn*ŭ et'ōōththŭ-th'ur*ayn*t'u-th'ŭ
Which do you prefer ?	niṅṅaḷkku ētāṇȧ pattyam ?	n'iṉgṉgu*l*kkŭ *ay*-th'*ahn*ŭ puththyam
No, thank you	vēṇṭa, dayavȧ	w*ayn*t'u, *th*uyawŭ
Help yourself	niṅṅaḷ eṭukkin	n'iṉgṉgu*l* et'ōōkkin
This is excellent	itȧ assal āyiṭṭuṇṭȧ; ita bēs āyiṭṭuṇṭȧ	ith'ŭ ussal *ah*yittōō*n*t'ŭ; ithŭ b*aysh* *ah*yittōō*n*t'ŭ
Change the plates	piññāṇam māṛuka	pi*nynyahn*um m*ah*ṛōōk'u
Give me a clean fork	enikku oru vṛtti-y-āya (nulla) muḷḷu tarika	enikkŭ orōō w*r*ththiy*ah*yu (n'ullu) mōō*ll*ŭ thurik'u
A clean knife	oru vṛitti-y-āya (nulla) katti	orōō w*r*ththiy*ah*yu (n'ullu) kuththi
Bring me a glass of water	enikku oru kḷāssȧ veḷḷam koṇṭuvannȧ tarika	enikkŭ orōō k*lah*ssŭ we*ll*um ko*n*t'ŭ-wun'n'ŭ thurik'u

English.	Malayalam.	Pronunciation.
Give me something to drink	enikku kuṭippān vallatum tarika	enikkŭ kōōt'ippahn wulluth'ōōm thurik'u

Tea (Eṭa-nēratte cāya).

English.	Malayalam.	Pronunciation.
Tea is ready	cāya tayyāṟ-āyi	chahyu thayyahṟ-ah-yi
Will you come ?	ninnaḷ varunnō ?	n'ingngul wurōōn'n'oh
Pour out the tea	cāya pakarnnȧ orikkuka	chahyu puk'urn'n'ŭ orikkōōk'u
Bring a saucer	oru aṭi-k-kiṇṇam koṇṭu-varika	orōō ut'i-k-kinnam kont'ŭ-wurik'u
Ring, if you please	dayavu ceytȧ, maṇi aṭikkuka	thuyawŭ cheyth'ŭ, muni ut'ikkōōk'u
A little more milk	kuṟaccu kūṭi pāl	kōōṟachchŭ koot'i pahl
More bread	kuṟe kūṭe ṟoṭṭi	kōōṟe koot'e ṟotti
A slice of bread and butter	oru kaṣṇam ṟoṭṭiyum, veṇṇayum	orōō kushnum ṟottiyōōm wennayōōm
Will you take some cake ?	ninnaḷ kuṟaccu appam kaṟikkunnō?	n'ingngul kōōṟachchu uppum kuṟikkōōn'n'oh
A small piece	oru ceṟiya kaṣṇam	orōō cheṟiyu kushnum
This is excellent tea	itȧ assal cāya	ith'ŭ ussal chahyu

Health (ārogyam, dēhasukam).

English.	Malayalam.	Pronunciation.
How are you ?	sukam tanneyō ?	sōōkum thunneyoh
I am very well	nalla sukam tanne	n'ullu sōōkum thunne
I am ill	enikku suka-k-kēṭȧ āṇȧ	enikkŭ sōōku-k-kayt'ŭ ahnŭ
I am not very well	enikku nalla sukam illa	enikkŭ n'ullu sōōkum illu
I hope you will soon be better	ninnaḷkku vēgam āśvāsam ākum ennu viśvasi-k-kunnu	n'ingngulkkŭ waygum ahswahsum ahkōōm en'n'ŭ wiswusi-k-kōōn'n'ōō

English.	Malayalam.	Pronunciation.
Do you sleep well ?	niṅṅalkku uṟakkam nallavaṇṇam uṇṭō ?	n'ingngu*l*kkŭ ōōṟakkum n'ulluwu*n*-*n*um ōō*nt'oh*
Pretty well, thank you	oru mātiri, dayavȧ	orōō m*ah*thiri, *th*ayuvŭ
I have caught a chill	enikku jaladōṣam piṭi-c-ciri-k-kunnu	enikkŭ jalu*thoh*shum pit'i-ch-chiri-k-kōōn'n'ōō
I feel sick	enikku manam peraṭṭunnu	enikkŭ munam perattōōn'n'ōō
Send for a doctor (native physician)	oru ḍākkaṭṭaṟkkȧ (vaidyannȧ) āḷayakkuka	orōō d*ah*kkuttŭṟkkŭ (w*ith*yannŭ) *ahl*uyakkōōk'u
I want to see a...	enikku oru ... kāṇēṇam ennuṇṭȧ	enikkŭ orōō ... k*ah*-*nayn*um en'n'ōō*n*-t'ŭ
She has a cough	avaḷkku oru cuma uṇṭȧ	uwu*l*kkŭ orōō chōōmu ōō*nt*'ŭ
Where is there a chemist's shop ?	oru marunnu ṣōppȧ eviṭe uṇṭȧ ?	orōō murōōn'n'ŭ sh*oh*ppŭ ewit'e ōō*nt*'ŭ
How much is the doctor's fee for a visit ?	ḍākkaṭṭaṟuṭe ōrō varavinnȧ entāṇa pīssȧ ?	d*ah*kkutturōōt'e *oh*-*roh* wuruwinnŭ en'th'*ahn*ŭ peessŭ
Have this prescription made up	ī kuṟippin pṟakāram marunnu kūṭṭi vekka	ee kōōṟippin pṟuk'*ah*rum murōōn'n'ŭ kootti wekku
One table-spoonful three times a day	oru mēśa-k-karaṇṭi vītam divasam mūnnu pṟāvaś—yam	orōō m*ay*su-k-kura*n*-t'i weeth'am *th*i-wusum moon'n'ŭ pṟ*ah*wusyam
To be taken after each meal	ōrō ūṇinnu śēṣavum kaṟippān	*ohroh* oo*n*innŭ *say*-shuwōōm kuṟip-p*ah*n
Shake the bottle	kuppi kulukkuka	kōōppi kōōlōōkkōōk'u
Outward application only	puṟattu piraṭṭān mātṟam	pōōruththŭ piratt-t*ah*n m*ah*thṟum

English.	Malayalam.	Pronunciation.
Poison	viṣam	wisham

The Time (samayam, nēram)

English.	Malayalam.	Pronunciation.
Please tell me the time	dayavu ceytá, etṟa maṇi-y-āyennu paṟayumō ?	*th*ayuvŭ cheyth'ŭ, ethṟu mu*n*i-y-*ah*yen'n'ŭ puṟayo͝o-mo*h*
What time is it ?	maṇi etṟa-y-āyi ?	mu*n*i ethṟu-y-*ah*yi
Ten minutes past seven	ēṟá aṭiccá pattá mi-niṭṭá	*ay*ṟŭ ut'ichchŭ puth-thŭ minittŭ
It has just struck nine	itā, ippōḷ ompatá aṭiccu	ith*ah*, ipp*ol* omp'u-th'ŭ ut'ichcho͝o
The clock is striking	maṇi aṭikkunnu	mu*n*i ut'ikko͝on'n'o͝o
A quarter past one	onnē-kālá	onn*ay*-k'*ah*lŭ
It is past one	oru maṇi kaṟiññirik-kunnu	oro͝o mu*n*i kuṟi*nyny*i-rikko͝on'n'o͝o
Half-past-four	nāl-ara	n*ah*l-uru
Twenty minutes to six	āṟ-aṭippān irupatu minittá	*ah*r-ut'ipp*ah*n iro͝o-puth'ŭ minittŭ
A quarter to eight	ēṟē-mukkāḷ	*ay*ṟ*ay*-mo͝okk*ah*l
By my watch	enṟe vāccu pṟakā-ram [yam	enṭe w*ah*chchŭ pṟu-k'*ah*ram [yam
Exactly 3 o'clock	mūnnu maṇi kṟt-	moon'n'ŭ mu*n*i k*r*th-
At what time ?	etṟa maṇikku ?	ethṟu mu*n*ikkŭ
9.0 a.m.	kālattu ompatu ma-ṇikká	k*ah*luththŭ omp'u-th'ŭ mu*n*ikkŭ
7.0 p.m.	vaikunnēram ēṟu maṇikká	w*i*ko͝on'n'*ay*rum *ay*-ṟŭ mu*n*ikkŭ
It is not late	vaikiyiṭ-ṭilla	w*i*kiyit-tillu
It is early	nēṟtte āṇá	n'*ay*ṟththe *ah*nŭ

Post-office and Telegrams

Tappālāppīsum Kampikaḷum.

English.	Malayalam.	Pronunciation.
Where is the telegraph (or post) office ?	kampi (tappāl) āp-pīsá eviṭe-y-āṇá ?	kump'i (thupp*ah*l) *ah*ppeesŭ ewit'e-y-*ah*nŭ

English.	Malayalam.	Pronunciation.
Have you any letters (telegrams, newspapers) for Mr. Smith ?	smit sāyvinȧ valla eṛuttukaḷ(kampikaḷ, vaṟtamāna-k-kaṭalāsukaḷ) uṇṭō ?	smith s*ah*ywinŭ wulla eṛōōththōōk'u*l* (kumpik'u*l*, wuṟtham*ah*nu-k-ku-t'al*ah*sōōk'u*l* ōō*n*-t'*oh*
Will this letter go to-night ?	ī eṛuttȧ innu rātṟi pōkumō ?	ee eṛōōththŭ in'n'ŭ r*ah*thṟi p*oh*k'ōō-m*oh*
I wish to send this to Mr. Brown	itȧ bṟauṇ sāyvinayappān āgrahikkunnu	ith'ŭ bṟ*own* s*ah*ywinuyapp*ah*n *ah*grahikkōōn'n'ōō
What is the postage of this letter ?	ī eṛuttinnȧ tappāl-k-kūli etṟa ?	ee eṛōōththinnŭ thupp*ah*l-k-kooli ethṟu
To register a letter	eṛuttȧ ṟajistṟākkuka	eṛōōththŭ ṟajisthṟ*ah*kkōōk'u
What is the charge?	kūli etṟa ?	kooli ethṟu
For the first ten words	ādyatte pattu vākkinȧ	*ah*thyaththe puththŭ w*ah*kkinŭ
For every additional word	kūṭutal ōrō vākkinum	koot'ōōth'ul *oh*r*oh* w*ah*kkinōōm
The name and address of sender	ayakkunna āḷuṭe pērum mēlvilāsavum	uyakkōōn'n'u *ah*lōō-ṭ'e p*ay*rōōm m*ay*lwil*ah*sawōōm
Reply paid	maṟuvaṭikkȧ muṅkūṟ aṭacca	muṟōōwat'ikkŭ mōōṉgk'ooṟ ut'-achchu
When is the next delivery ?	iniyatte tappāl varavȧ eppoṟāṇȧ ?	iniyaththe thupp*ah*l wuruwŭ eppoṟah-*n*ŭ
When does the post-office close ?	tappālāppisȧ eppoṟaṇȧ pūṭṭunnatȧ?	thupp*ah*l*ah*ppeesŭ eppoṟ*ah*nŭ poot-tōōn'n'uth'ŭ
I want a money-order for...	...kkȧ oru maṇiyōṟḍaṟ vēṇam	...kkŭ orōō mu*n*iy*oh*ṟdŭṟ way*n*um
Payable at...	...il koṭuppānuḷḷa	...il kot'ōōpp*ah*nōō*ll*u

English.	Malayalam.	Pronunciation.
Is the English mail in yet ?	bilāttiyil ninnuḷḷa tappāl vannirikkunnō ?	bil*ah*ththiyil n'in'n'ōō*ll*u thupp*ah*l wun'n'irikkōōn'n'*oh*
The last delivery is at...o'clock	oṭuvilatte tappāl varavȧ ... maṇikkāṇȧ	ot'ōōwilaththe thupp*ah*l wuruwŭ ... mu*n*ikk*ahn*ŭ

In Town (Paṭṭaṇattil).

English.	Malayalam.	Pronunciation.
Where shall we go ?	nām eviṭekkāṇu pōkēṇṭatȧ ?	n'*ah*m ewit'ekk*ahn*ŭ pohk'*ayn*t'uth'ŭ
Let us go	namukku pōkam	n'umōōkkŭ p*oh*k'*ah*m
Which is the way to... ?	...kku vaṛi ētāṇȧ ?	...kkŭ wuṛi *ay*th'*ah*nŭ
Where does this road lead to ?	ī vaṛi eviṭekkāṇȧ pokunnatȧ ?	ee wuṛi ewit'ekk*ahn*ŭ p*oh*kōōn'n'uth'ŭ
Go up the street	teruvinṟe aṅṅet-talakkalēkku naṭakkuka	therōōwinṯe uṉgṉgeth-thulakkulakkŭ nut'ukkōōk'u
Is it far from here ?	atȧ iviṭunnȧ dūrattāṇō ?	uth'ŭ iwit'ōōn'n'ŭ *th*oorathth*ahnoh*
How far is it to... ?	...kku entu dūram uṇṭȧ ?	...kkŭ en'th'ŭ *th*ooram ōōnt'ŭ
Show me the way	enikku vaṛi kāṭṭi-t-tarāmō	enikkŭ wuṛi k*ah*tti-th-thur*ah*m*oh*
Turn to the right	valattōṭṭu tiriyuka	wulaththo*h*ttŭ thiriyōōk'u
Go quickly	vēgam pōkuka	waygum p*oh*k'ōōk'u
— slowly	patukke pōkuka	puth'ōōkke p*oh*k'ōōk'u
— straight	nērē pōkuka	n*av*r*ay* p*oh*k'ōōk'u
Keep to the left	iṭat-taṭuttȧ pōkuka	it'aththut'ōōththŭ p*oh*k'ōōk'u
Second turning to the right	valattu bāgam raṇṭām tirivȧ	wulaththŭ b*ah*gam ru*n*t'*ah*m thiriwȧ

English.	Malayalam.	Pronunciation.
Take the first to the left and the second to the right	iṭattu bāgam ādyatte tirivȧ eṭuttȧ, pinne valattu bagam ranṭām tirivȧ eṭukkuka	it'aththŭ b*ah*gam *ahth*yaththe thiriwȧ et'o͝oththŭ, pinne wulaththŭ b*ah*gam ru*nt'ah*m thiriwȧ et'o͝okko͝ok'u
Cross the road	vaṟi vilaṇṇane kaṭakkuka	wuri wilangngane kut'ukko͝ok'u
In what street is...?	...ētu teruvilāṇȧ uḷḷatȧ ?	...*ay*th'ŭ thero͝owi*lahn*o͝o*ll*uth'ŭ
Please direct me the nearest way to:..	...kku ēṟṟavum curuṅṅiya vaṟi kāṭṭittannāl koḷḷām	...kkŭ *ay*ṯṯuwo͝om cho͝oro͝ongngiyu wuṟi k*ah*ttiththun'n'*ah*l ko*ll*ahm
Is this the way to...?	...kku itāṇō vaṟi ?	...kkŭ ith'*ahnoh* wuri ?
Do you know Mr. F.	F. sāyvine aṟiyumō	F. s*ah*ywine uṟiyo͝omoh
I don't know anyone of that name	ā pēruḷḷa ārēyum ñān aṟiyilla	*ah* payroo*ll*u *ahray*yo͝om *nyah*n uṟiyillu
I know him very well	enikku addēhamāyiṭṭȧ nalla paricayam uṇṭȧ	enikkŭ u*ththay*hum*ah*yittŭ n'ullu purich'uyam o͝o*n*t'ŭ
Who is he ?	addēham ārāṇȧ ?	u*ththay*hum *ahrah*nŭ ?
He is an old friend of mine	addēham enṟe oru paṟaya snēhitan āṇȧ	u*ththay*hum enṯe oro͝o puṟayu sn'*ay*hith'an *ah*nŭ
Where does he live ?	addēhattinṟe tāmasam eviṭe ?	u*ththay*huththinṯe th*ah*musum ewit'e ?
Close by (me)	(enikku) aṭuttu tanne	(enikkŭ) ut'o͝oththŭ thunne
Can you take me to a good hotel ?	oru nalla hōṭṭalilekku ennē kūtti-k-koṇṭu pōkāmō ?	oro͝o n'ullu h*oh*ttalilekkŭ enn*ay* koott-i-k-ko*n*t'o͝o *poh*k'*ah*m*oh* ?

English.	Malayalam.	Pronunciation.
Is Mr. F. (Mrs. F.) at home ?	F. sāyvȧ (F. madāmma) vīṭṭil uṇṭō ?	F. *sah*ywŭ (F. mu*thah*mmu) weettil *oo*n*t'oh?*
Good morning	suprabātam	sooprub*ah*th'um
How do you do ?	sukam tannayō ?	sookum thunnay*oh*
Very well	nalla sukam tanne [tanne	n'ullu sookum thunne [thunne
I am very well	enikku nalla sukam	enikkŭ n'ullu sookum
I must go	enikku pōṇam	enikkŭ p*ohn*um
Good-bye, farewell	salām, pinne kāṇām	sul*ah*m, pinne *kahnah*m
I wish you good morning	ñān niṅṅaḷkku salām parayunnu	*nyah*n n'ingngal*l*kkŭ ? sul*ah*m purayoon'n'oo [num
Good evening	sāyānha vandanam	s*ah*y*ah*nhu wun'*tha*-
Good night	niśā „	n'is*ah* „
What is the name of that village ?	ā grāmattinṟe pērȧ entaṇȧ ?	*ah* gr*ah*maththinte p*ay*rŭ en'th'*ah*nŭ ?
What sort of a road is it ?	atȧ entumātiri - y - oru vari āṇȧ ?	uth'ŭ en'th'oom*ah*th'iri-y-oroo wuri *ah*nŭ ?
Which way am I to go ?	ñaṉ ētu variyē-y-aṇȧ pōkēṇṭatȧ ?	*nyah*n *ay*th'ŭ wuriyay-y-*ah*nŭ p*oh*k*ayn*t'uth'ŭ
You are in the right way	niṅṅaḷ śari variyē-y-aṇȧ pōkunnatȧ	n'ingngul *s*ariwuriyay-y*ahn*ŭ p*oh*k'oon'n'uth'ŭ
You are quite out of the way	niṅṅaḷkku vallāte vari terrip-pōyi	ningngul*l*kkŭ wull*ah*th'e wuri thettipp*oh*yi
Have you a card ?	niṅṅaḷuṭe pēruḷḷa oru kārḍȧ uṇṭō ?	n'ingngul*l*oot'e p*ay*rool*l*u oroo *kah*rdŭ oo*nt'oh?*
Give him my card	enṟe pēruḷḷa kārḍȧ addēhattinnu koṭukkuka	ente p*ay*rool*l*u *kah*rdŭ u*ththay*huththinnŭ kot'ookkook'u

English.	Malayalam.	Pronunciation.
I will call again	ñān iniyum orikkal varām	nyahn iniyo͝om orikkal wurahm
Does he expect you?	addēham niṅṅaḷkku vēṇṭi kāttirikkunnuṇṭō ?	uththayhum ningngulkkŭ waynt'i kahththirikko͝on'n'oont'oh?
He is expecting you	addēham niṅṅaḷe kāttirikkayāṇá	uththayhum n'ingngule kahththirikkayahnŭ
I have an engagement with him	enikku addēhavumāyi oru sandarśanattinná ērppāṭá uṇṭá	enikkŭ uththayhuwo͝omahyi oro͝o sun'thursanuththinnŭ ayrpaht'ŭ o͝ont'ŭ

Shopping (sāmānam vāṅṅal)

English.	Malayalam.	Pronunciation.
How much ?	etra ?	ethru ?
That is too much	atá vaḷare jāsti	uth'ŭ wulare jahsth'i
What is the price ?	entā vila ?	en'th'ah wilu
Will you send them at once ?	avaye uṭane ayakkāmō ?	uwaye o͝ot'ane uyakkahmoh
I wish to buy...	...vāṅṅuvān vicārikkunnu	...wahngngo͝owahn wichahrikko͝on'n'o͝o
I will take this	ñān itāṇá eṭukkunnatá	nyahn ith'ahnŭ et'o͝okko͝on'n'uth'ŭ
Send them to...	...kku ayakkuka	...kkŭ uyakko͝ok'u
I want some calico	enikku kuṟaccu kālikkōttuṇi vēṇam	enikkŭ ko͝orachchŭ kahlikkohththo͝oni waynam
I should like to see some ribbons	kuṟe paṭṭu-nāṭattaraṅṅaḷ kaṇṭāl koḷḷāmennuṇṭá	ko͝ore putto͝o-nah-t'uth-thurangngul kunt'ahl kollahmen'n'o͝ont'ŭ

English.	Malayalam.	Pronunciation.
This colour is too dark (-light)	ī niṟam vallāte kaṭun-niṟam (-lagu) āyippōyi	ee niṟam wull*ah*th'e kuto͝on'-n'iṟam (-lago͝o) *ah*yipp*oh*yi
Have you any narrower (-broader)	itilum vīti kuṟañña kūṭiya) vallatum uṇṭō ?	ith'ilo͝om weeth'i ko͝oṟa*nyny*u (koot'iyu) wullath'o͝om o͝o*nt'oh*
What is this, a yard ?	itȧ etṟa, oru vāṟayō ?	ith'ŭ ethṟu, oro͝o w*ah*ṟay*oh*
It is faded	atȧ niṟam maṅṅiyatȧ āṇȧ	uth'ŭ n'iṟam muṉgṉgiyath'ŭ *ah*ṉŭ
Not so fine	atṟa nēṟttatu vēṇṭa	uthṟu n*ay*ṟthath'u w*ay*nt'u
This will do	itȧ mati	ith'ŭ muth'i
A skein of sewing silk	oru curuḷ paṭṭu tunnanūlȧ	orŭ cho͝oro͝o*l* puttŭ tho͝onnun'oolŭ
What are they a pair ?	oru jōṭikku etṟa ?	oro͝o j*oh*t'ikkŭ ethṟu
It is too dear	atinu vallātta vila	uth'inŭ wull*ah*ththa wilu
Is this cheap ?	itinu sahāyam uṇṭō ?	ith'inŭ suh*ah*yam o͝o*nt'oh*
Try on these	iva iṭṭu nōkku	iwu ittŭ n'*oh*kko͝o
They fit you very well	ava niṅṅaḷkku nallavaṇṇam yōjiccirikkunnu	uwu n'iṉgṉgu*l*kkŭ n'ulluwu*nn*am y*oh*jichchirikko͝on'n'o͝o
I shall take them with me	avaye enṟe kūṭe eṭuttu koḷḷām	uwaye enṯe koot'e et'o͝oththo͝o ko*l*-*lah*m
Make out my bill	enṟe (kaṇakku) billu taru	enṯe (ku*n*akkŭ) billŭ thuro͝o

Shooting (nāyāṭṭȧ)

Have I to obtain permission to shoot here ?	iviṭe veṭi-vekkuvān anuvādam vāṅṅēṇṭa āvaśyam uṇṭō ?	iwit'e wet'i-wekko͝ow*ah*n uno͝ow*ah*tham w*ah*ṉgṉg*ay*nt'u *ah*wasyum o͝o*nt'oh*

English.	Malayalam.	Pronunciation.
To whom must I apply ?	ārōṭāṇā apēkṣikkēṇṭatā ?	*ah*roh*t*'*ah*nŭ up'*ayk*'shikk*aynt*'ath'ŭ
What kind of game can I get here ?	iviṭe entellām taram mṛgaṅṅaḷe-k-kiṭṭum ?	iwite en'th'ell*ah*m thuram m*r*guṇgṇgu*le*-k-kitto͞om
Elk, deer, hare, wild buffalo, boar, fox tiger, elephant, &c.	mala-mān, mān, muyal, kāṭṭu-pōttā kāṭṭu-panni, kuṟukkan, nari, āna, mutalāyava	mulum*ah*n, m*ah*n, mo͞oyal, k*ah*ttŭ-p*oh*ththŭ, k*ah*ttŭ-pun'n'i, ko͞oṟo͞okkun, n'uri, *ah*nu, mo͞oth'al*ah*yawu
Can I obtain the exclusive right to the shooting ?	veṭi-vekkuvān uḷḷa adikāram enikku mātṟamay-k-kiṭṭuvān sādyamō ?	wet'i wekko͞ow*ah*n o͞o*ll*u u*th*ik*ah*ram enikkŭ m*ah*thram*ah*y-k-kitto͞ow*ah*n sah*th*yam*oh*
What rent must I pay ?	entu kūli (vāṭaka) koṭukkēṇṭi varum ?	en'th'ŭ kooli (w*ah*t'ak'u) koto͞okk*ayn*t'i wuro͞om
Can I get one or two experienced men to go out shooting with me ?	onnu raṇṭu veṭi-veccu taṟakkamuḷḷavare enṟe kuṭe varuvān kiṭṭumō ?	onnŭ ru*n*t'ŭ wet'i-wechchŭ thuṟakkum-o͞o*ll*uwure enṭe koot'e wuro͞ow*ah*n kitto͞omoh
How much must I pay each of them per day (week) ?	avaril ōrōruttannum divasam (āṟca) entu vītam koṭukkēṇṭi varum ?	uwuril *oh*r*oh*ro͞oththanno͞om *th*iwasum (*ah*ṟchu) en'th'ŭ weeth'am kot'o͞okk*ayn*t'i wuro͞om
How many dogs can you let me have ?	etṟa nāy-k-kaḷe enikku taruvān sadikkum ?	ethṟu n'*ah*y-k-ku*le* enikkŭ thuro͞ow*ah*n s*ah*th*ik*ko͞om
Are the dogs properly trained ?	śariyāy śilippic-ciṭṭuḷḷa nāy-k-kaḷāṇō ?	sariy*ah*y seelippichchitto͞o*ll*u n'*ah*y-k-ku*lah*n*oh*

English.	Malayalam.	Pronunciation.
Keep the dogs back	nāy-k-kaḷe pinnākkam niṟtuka	n'*ah*y-k-ku*le* pin*nah*kkum n'iṟtho͝ok'u
Load my gun	enṟe tōkkil marunnu niṟakkuka	enṯe tho*h*kkil muro͝on'n'ŭ n'iṟakko͝ok'u
Carry my gun	enṟe tōkkȧ cumakkuka	enṯe tho*h*kkŭ chumukko͝ok'u
Give me some cartridges	enikku kuṟe tōṭṭa tarika	enikkŭ ko͝oṟe tho*h*ttu thurik'u
Do not fire!	veṭi vekkarutȧ	wet'i wekkaro͝oth'ŭ
Let me have a shot with your gun	niṅṅaḷuṭe tōkku koṇṭȧ oru veṭi vekkaṭṭe	ningngu*l*o͝ot'e tho*h*kkŭ ko*n*t'ŭ oro͝o wet'i wekkatte
To cock a gun	tōkkȧ ceṟukkuka (or paṟikkuka)	tho*h*kkŭ cheṟo͝okko͝ok'u (*or* puṟikko͝oku)

Fishing (Matsyam piṭikkal)

Is there any fishing to be had near here?	iviṭaṅṅaḷil matsyam piṭikkān saukaryam uṇṭō?	iwit'angngu*l*il mulsyam pit'ikk*ah*n *sow*k'uryam o͝o*n*t'*oh*
Must I first obtain permission to fish?	matsyam piṭikkān ādyamāyi sammatam vāṅṅēṇṭa-tuṇṭō?	mulsyam pit'ikk*ah*n *ah*thyam*ah*yi summuth'um wahngng*ayn*t'a-th'o͝o*n*t'*oh*
What is the rent for fishing in this river (lake, pond)	ī puṟayil (taṭākattil, kuḷattil) matsyam piṭikkān entāṇu kūli?	ee po͝oṟayil (thut'*ah*k'uththil, ko͝o*l*uththil) mulsyam pit'ikk*ah*n en'th'*ah**n*ŭ kooli
Can I get the sole right of fishing?	matsyam piṭikkānuḷḷa avakāśam enikku mātṟamāy-k-kiṭṭuvān sādyamō?	mulsyam pit'ikk*ah*no͝o*ll*u uwuk'*ah*sum enikkŭ m*ah*thṟam*ah*y-k-kitto͝ow*ah*n s*ahth*yam*oh*

English.	Malayalam.	Pronunciation.
Can I have a boat and man ?	oru vañciyum āḷum kiṭṭumō ?	oroo wunych'iyoom *ahl*oom kittoo-m*oh*
What do you charge for the hour (day)	maṇikkūṟinnȧ (divasam) niṅṅaḷkkȧ entu vītam kūli tarēṇṭi varum ?	mu*n*ikkooṟinne (*thi*wasum) n'iṉgṉgu*l*kkŭ en'th'oo weeth'am kooli thu*rayn*t'i wuroom
Are you an experienced fisherman?	niṅṅaḷkku matsyam piṭiccu taṟakkam (śīlam) uṇṭō ?	n'iṉgṉgu*l*kkŭ mulsyam pit'ichchŭ thuṟukkum (*s*eelam) oo*n*t'*oh*
Can I depend on you ?	enikku niṅṅaḷil viśvāsam vekkāmō ?	enikkŭ n'iṉgṉgu*l*il wisw*ah*sum wekk*ah*m*oh*
The oar	tanṭȧ ; paṅkāyam	thu*n*t'ŭ ; puṉgk'*ah*yam
Have you brought some bait ?	niṅṅal kuṟaccȧ ira koṇṭu vanniṭṭuṇṭō ?	niṉgṉgul kooṟachchŭ iru ko*n*t'oo wun'n'ittoo*n*t*oh*
What bait must I use ?	ñān entȧ irayāṇȧ upayōgik-kēṇṭatȧ ?	*nyah*n en'th'ŭ iru*yah*nŭ oop'ay*oh*gik-k*ayn*t'ath'ŭ
Will you bring bait ?	ira koṇṭu warāmō ?	iru ko*n*t'oo wur*ah*m*oh*
Give me a hook	oru kokki (koḷuttȧ) taru	oroo kokki (ko*l*ooththŭ) thuroo
Will you bait my line ?	enṟe kokkiyin-mēl ira koḷutti-t-tarumō ?	enṯe kokkiyin-m*ay*l iru ko*l*ooththi-th-thuroom*oh*
Give me my rod	enṟe cūṇṭal-vaṭi taru	enṯe choo*n*t'al-wut'i thuroo
Row gently	patukke taṇṭu-valikku	puth'ookke thu*n*t'oo wulikkoo
Do not make a noise	occa iṭarutȧ ; (or, sabdam uṇṭākkarutȧ)	ochcha it'urooth'ŭ ; (*or* sub*th*um oo*n*t'*ah*kkurath'ŭ)

English.	Malayalam.	Pronunciation.
Make haste	dṛti vekku	*thr*th'i wekko͞o
The fishing is good here	iviṭam matsyam pitikkān nalla dikkȧ ānȧ	iwit'am mulsyam pit'ikk*ah*n n'ullu *th*ikkŭ *ah*nŭ
How much does this fish weigh?	ī matsyattinnȧ entu tūkkam uṇṭȧ?	ee mulsyaththinnŭ en'th'ŭ thookkum o͞o*nt*'ŭ [k*ah*m*oh*
Will you weigh it?	atȧ tūkki nōkkāmō?	uthŭ thookki n*oh*k-

Commercial and Trading (kaccavaṭa-k-kāryam)

English.	Malayalam.	Pronunciation.
Send in my account	enṟe kaṇakkȧ ayakkuka	enṯe kunakkŭ uyakko͞oku
I am leaving tomorrow	ñān nāḷe pōka-y-āṇȧ	*nyah*n n'*ah*l*e* p*oh*k'a-y-*ah*nŭ
You have overcharged me	niṅṅaḷ enne adikac-cārjȧ ceytirikkunnu	ningngu*l* enne ¦u*thi*ku-ch-ch*ah*ṟjŭ cheyth'irikko͞on'n'o͞o
Give me a receipt	enikku oru raśīti taru	enikkŭ orŭ raseeth'i thuro͞o
That firm has failed	ā kaccavaṭakkāṟ poliññu poyirikkunnu	*ah* kuchchawut'ukk*ah*ṟ po*li*ny*ny*ŭ p*oh*y-irikko͞on'n'o͞o
What are the assets?	entokkayāṇȧ mutalȧ?	en'th'okka-y-*ah*nŭ mo͞oth'alŭ
Show me a balance sheet	enikku oru bākkittaḷḷal paṭṭika kāṭṭi-t-taru	enikkŭ oro͞o b*ah*kki-th-thu*ll*ul puttiku k*ah*tti-th-thuro͞o
What are the liabilities?	kaṭaṅṅaḷ entokka?	kut'angngu*l* en'thokku
There is an error in your account	niṅṅaḷuṭe kaṇakkil oru teṟṟuṇṭȧ	ningngu*l*o͞ot'e ku*n*akkil oro͞o theṯto͞o*nt*'ŭ
My samples are delayed	enṟe māṯṟkakaḷ varuvān vaikiyi-y-irikkunnu	enṯe m*ah*th*r*k'uk'u*l* wuro͞ow*ah*n w*i*k'i-yirikko͞on'n'o͞o

English.	Malayalam.	Pronunciation.
I want to get them through the Custom House	avaye cuṅka-p-purayil kūṭe pāssākki-k-kiṭṭuvān ñān āvaśya-p-peṭunnu	uwaye chōōṉgk'uppōōrayil koote pahssahkki-k-kittōōwahn nvahn ahwasyup-pet'ōōn' n'ōō
I want a detailed statement	enikku oru inam inam āya vivaraṇam vēṇam	enikkŭ orōō inam inam ahyu wiwarunum waynum
I shall send in a claim	ñan oru avakāśa-k-kaippīttȧ ayakkum	nyahn orōō uwak'ahṣu-k-kippeeththŭ uyakkōōm
Can I insure my luggage ?	enṟe sāmānam inṣuvaṟ ceyyān sādyamo ?	enṯe sahmahnam inshōōwuṟ cheyyahn sahthyamoh
What is the rate ?	entā nirakkȧ ?	en'th'ah n'irakkŭ
What is the charge?	kūli entāṇȧ ?	kooli en'th'ahnŭ
Will you accept a bill ?	niṅṅaḷ oru billu (huṇṭi) svīkarikkumō ?	niṉgṉgul orōō billŭ (hōōnt'i) sweek'urikkōōmoh
At three months	mūnnu māsattil	moon'n'ŭ mahsaththil
Send by fast train	vēga-vaṇṭi vaṟiyāy ayakkuka	waygu-wunt'i wuṟiyahy uyakkōōk'u
They can go by goods train	avaye sāmāna-vaṇṭi vaṟiyāy ayakkān sādikkum	uwaye sahmahnuwunt'i wuṟiyahy uyakkahn sahthikkōōm
What dividend has been declared ?	etṟa-y-āṇȧ lāba-vītam niścayicciṭṭuḷḷatȧ ?	ethṟeyahnŭ lahbuweeth'um n'ischayichchit-tōōllath'-ŭ
Your luggage is liable to duty	niṅṅaḷuṭe sāmānattinmēl cuṅkam cumattēṇṭatȧ āṇȧ	niṉgṉgulōōt'e sahmahnaththinmayl chōōṉgk'um chōōmuththaynt'uth'u ahnŭ

English.	Malayalam.	Pronunciation.
This cheque needs endorsing	ī cekkin-purattȧ oppiṭēṇṭatȧ āṇȧ	ee chekkin-pōōrath-thŭ oppit'aynt'u-th'ŭ ahnŭ
Have you declared the value ?	vilakku mori koṭu-ttiṭ-ṭuṇṭō ?	wilakkŭ mori kot'ōō-ththit-tōōnt'oh
I will prepay the carriage	cumaṭṭu-kūli muṅ-kūrāy koṭukkām	chōōmuttŭ kooli mōōngk'oorahy kot'ōōkkahm
I have a letter of introduction	paricayap-peṭut-tum kattȧ onnȧ enre vaśam uṇṭȧ	purich'ayup-pe-t'ōōththōōm kuth-thŭ on'n'ŭ ente wu sum ōōnt'ŭ
Give me your estimate	niṅṅaḷ oru kaṁma-tik-kaṇakku (ud-dēśak-kaṇakku) taru	ningngul orōō kum-math'i-k-kunukkŭ (ōōth-thaysu-k-kunukkŭ) thurōō
Quote me a price	oru vila parayu	orōō wilu purayōō

Public Works (Marāmattȧ)

Come here with your hoe	kaikkōṭṭum koṇṭȧ iviṭe varu	kikkohttōōm kont'ŭ iwit'e wurōō
Bring (it) here	iviṭekku koṇṭu-va-ru	iwit'ekkŭ kontŭ-wu-rōō [th'ŭ
Don't dig there	aviṭe kiḷakkarutȧ	uwit'e kilakkurōō-
Dig wider	kure-k-kūṭe vistā-ramāy kiḷakkuka	kōōre-k-koot'e wis-thahramahy ki-lakkōōk'u
How many men are wanted to cut the jungle ?	kāṭu veṭṭuvān etra āḷe āvaśyam uṇ-ṭȧ ?	kaht'ŭ wettōōwahn ethru ahle ahwas-yum ōōnt'ŭ
Six men are wanted for road work	pātamēl vēlakkȧ ār-āḷe āvaśyam uṇ-ṭȧ	pahth'umayl waylak-kŭ ahr-ahle ahwas-yum ōōnt'ŭ
Send three men to help the carpenters	āśārimāre sahāyik-kān mūn-nāḷe a-yakkuka	ahsahrimahre suhah-yikkahn moon'-n'ahle uyakkōōk'u

English.	Malayalam.	Pronunciation.
Take six men to build the bridge	pālam paṇiyuvān āṟ-āḷe eṭuttu koḷ-ḷu	pahlam puniyoowahn ahrahle et'ooththũ kolloo
What kind of soil is there at that place ?	ā dikkil entu taram maṇṇāṇȧ uḷḷatȧ?	ah thikkil en'thũ thuram munnah-nũ oollath'ŭ
Very sandy	vallātta maṇal pṟa-dēśam āṇȧ	wullahththu munal-pruthaysum ahnũ
Where was this stiff clay got ?	ī kaṭṭi-k-kaḷimaṇ-ṇu eviṭe ninnānȧ kiṭṭiyatȧ ?	ee kutti-k-kulimun-nũ ewit'e n'in'n'ah nũ kittiyath'ŭ
This is exceedingly hard ground	itu vallāte uṟacca būmi tanne	ith'ŭ wullahth'e oo-rachchu boomi th'unne
The hoe will break	kaikkōttu muṟiññu (or oṭiññu) pō-kum	kikkohttũ mooriny-nyũ (or ot'inynyũ) pohk'oom
A pick-axe will be required here	iviṭe oru pikkāssu tanne veṇṭi va-rum	iwit'e oroo pikkahssũ thunne waynt'i wuroom
Remove the stones with a crow-bar	kallukaḷ oru iḷavāṅ-ku kontȧ nīkku-ka	kullook'ul oroo ilu-wahngk'oo kont'ŭ n'eekkook'u
Blast out this rock	pāṟa veṭi veccu nīk-ku	pahru wet'i wechchũ n'eekkoo
Put aside all stones suitable for the foundation	astivārattinnu tak-katāya ellā kallu-kaḷum oru bāga-t-tiṭuka	usthiwahraththinnũ thukk'uthahyu el-lah kullook'uloom o-roo bahgu-th-thi-t'ook'u
The space is not suf-ficient	stalam pōra	sthulam pohru
Measure a foot and a half	onnara aṭi aḷakku-ka	on'n'aru ut'i uluk-kook'u
Level thirty feet fur-ther back	iniyum muppatȧ aṭi pinnākkam nikat tuka	iniyoom moopputh'ŭ ut'i pinnahkkum n'ik'uththook'u

English.	Malayalam.	Pronunciation.
The ground is very soft ; you must therefore lay a plank	nilam vaḷure catup-puḷḷatāṇȧ ; atu-koṇṭȧ oru palaka vekkēṇṭi varum	n'ilum wu*l*ure chu th'ŏŏp-pŏŏ*ll*uth'-*ahn*ŭ ; uth'ŏŏk'*on*-t'ŭ orŏŏ pulak'u wekk*aynt*'i wu-rŏŏm
Come this way ; this ground is harder	itile varu ; iviṭe ni-lam adikam uṟap puḷḷatāṇȧ	ith'ile wurŏŏ ; iwit'e n'ilam u*th*ik am ŏŏrappŏŏ*ll*uth'*ah*-*n*ŭ
Bring the line and pegs to mark out the foundation	astivāram varakku-vān kayaṟum kuṟ-ṟikaḷum koṇṭu-varika	usthiw*ah*ram wurak-kŏŏw*ah*n kuya-ṟŏŏm kŏŏṯṯik'u-*l*ŏŏm ko*n*t'ŭ wuri-k'u
Must this work be done to-day ?	ī paṇi innu tīṟkkē-ṇamō ?	ee pu*n*i in'n'ŭ theeṟk kay*n*am*oh*
How do you ar-range the bricks in this kiln ?	ī cūḷayil iṣṭakakaḷ niṅṅaḷ eṅṅineyā-ṇȧ aṭukkuka ?	ee choo*l*ayil ishtak'u-ku*l* n'iṉgṉgu*l* eṉg-ṉgineyah*n*ŭ u-t'ŏŏkkŏŏk'u
I want to build a house	ñān oru vīṭu paṇi-yēṇam ennu vi-cārikkunnu	*nyah*n orŏŏ weet'ŭ pu*n*iy*ayn*am en'-n'ŭ vich*ah*rik-kŏŏn'n'ŏŏ
Will you bring me an estimate ?	oru kammati ka-ṇakku koṇṭuva-rāmō ?	orŏŏ kummuth'i ku-*n*ukkŭ ko*n*t'ŭ wu-r*ah*m*oh*
Your estimate is too high	niṅṅaḷuṭe kammati jāsti āyip-pōyi	niṉgṉgu*l*ŏŏt'e kum-muth'i j*ah*sthi ah-yip-p*oh*yi
I shall come fre-quently and see how the work is progressing	ñān kūṭekkūṭe van-nȧ paṇi eṅṅine naṭannu varuṇu ennu nōkkunna-tāṇȧ	*nyah*n koot'ekkoot'e wun'n'ŭ pu*n*i eṉg-ṉgine n'ut'an'n'ŭ wurŏŏ*n*ŏŏ en'n'ŭ n'*oh*kkŏŏn'n'ath'-*ahn*ŭ

English.	Malayalam.	Pronunciation.
There is not enough sand in this mortar	ī kummāyattil maṇal pōra	ee kōōmmahyaththil mu*n*ul pohru
The foundation must be compact and strong	astivārattinnȧ otukkavum balavum vēṇam	usthiw*ah*raththinnū oth'ōōkkuwōōm buluwōōm w*ayn*am
You are wasting lime	niṅṅaḷ ittiḷȧ (kummāyam) verute kaḷakayāṇȧ	ningngu*l* iththi*l*ū kōōmm*ah*yam werōōth'e ku*l*ak'uy*ahn*ū
Let the doors and windows be well-fitted	vātilukaḷum, janērikaḷum nallavaṇṇam uṟappikkaṭṭe	w*ah*th'ilōōk'u*l*ōōm, jun*ay*rik'u*l*ōōm n'ulluwu*nn*um ōōruppikkutte
The plastering of the wall must be done neatly	cumaru parukkan tēkkunnatȧ vṛttiyāyi vēnam	chōōmarū purōōkkan th*ay*ykkōōn'n'uth'ū w*r*ththiy*ah*yi w*ayn*um
White ants will attack the timber ; tar it	maram citalȧ piṭikkum ; kīl iṭuka	muram chith'alū pit'ikkōōm ; keel it'ōōk'u
These tiles are not good	ī ōṭukaḷ nalla-t-alla	ee *oh*t'ōōk'u*l* n'ullath'ullu
If a heavy shower of rain falls many of the tiles will be destroyed	oru nalla maṛa peytāl ōṭukaḷil anavadi uṭaññu naṣṭamāy-p-pōkum	orōō n'ullu muru peyth'*ah*l *oh*t'ōōk'u*l*il unavu*th*i ōōt'*any*nyū n'ushtum*ah*y-p-p*oh*k'ōōm
Thatch the roof	(mēl-) pura mēyuka	(m*ay*l-) pōōru m*ay*yōōk'u
Is the thatch ready ?	mēyuvān vaikkōlȧ (ōla) tayyāṟuṇṭō?	m*ay*yōōw*ah*n w*i*kk*oh*lū (*oh*lu) th'ay-y*ah*rōō*n*t'*oh*
Fasten it firmly	atȧ uṟappāy keṭṭuka	uth'ū ōōrapp*ah*y kettōōk'u
Tar the floor	nilam kīl iṭuka	n'ilam keel it'ook'u -

English.	Malayalam.	Pronunciation.
Put cement over it	atin-mēle śīma-k-kummāyam tēk-kuka	uth'in-m*ay*le seema-k-kōōmm*ah*yam th*ay*kkōōk'u
Lay large stones a-cross	valiya kallukaḷ vi-laṅṅane vekkuka	wuliya kullōōku*l* wi-laṉgṉgune wekkōō-k'u
Bring the chain	caṅṅala koṇṭu-va-rika	chuṉgṉgalu ko*n*t'ŭ-wurik'u
Hold your pole in a line with the theodolite and the other pole	niṅṅaḷuṭe muḷavaṭi tiyōḍalaiṟṟinnum maṟṟe muḷava-ṭikkum nēre oru variyāy piṭikku-ka	n'iṉgṉgu*l*ōōte mōō-*l*uwut'i thiyo*h*da-liṯṯinnōōm muṯṯe moo*l*uwut'ikkōōm n'*ay*re orōō wuri-y*ah*y pit'ikkōōk'u
Take the chain and iron pegs, and go there	caṅṅalayum irum-pu kuṟṟikaḷum e-ṭuttā aviṭe pōka	chuṉgṉgulayōōm i-rōōmp'ŭ kōōṯṯiku-*l*ōōm et'ōōththŭ u-wit'e po*h*k'u
Where are the iron pegs?	irumpu kuṟṟikaḷ e-viṭe?	irōōmp'ŭ kōōṯṯik'u*l* ewit'e
You go in the direc-tion of that flag, and put down pegs	ā koṭikku nēre pōyi kuṟṟikaḷ aṭikku-ka	*ah* kot'ikkŭ n'*ay*re po*h*yi kōōṯṯiku*l* u-t'ikkōōk'u

Planting (Tōṭṭa-p-paṇi)

English.	Malayalam.	Pronunciation.
How many coolies have you?	niṅṅaḷute kīḻil etṟa kūlikkāṟ uṇṭā?	niṉgṉgu*l*ōōt'e keeṟil ethṟu koolikk*ah*ṟ ōō*n*t'ŭ
How many of them are women and children?	avaril stṟīkaḷum kuṭṭikaḷum etṟa pēṟ?	uwaril sthṟeek'u*l*ōōm kōōttiku*l*ōōm eth-ṟu payṟ
How long have they been with you?	avaṟ niṅṅaḷuṭe kū-ṭe āyiṭṭu etṟa kā-lamāyi?	uwaṟ niṉgṉgu*l*ōōt'e koot'e *ah*yittŭ eth-ṟu k*ah*lumahyi
Are they good workers?	avaṟ nalla paṇikkā-rō?	uwar n'ullu pu*n*ik-k*ah*r*ho*

English.	Malayalam.	Pronunciation.
If you work for me you must be diligent, orderly and obedient	enṟe kiṟil vēla ceykayāṇeṅkil, utsāhavum, maryādayum, anusaraṇavum vēṇam	enṯe keeṟil waylu cheykay*ahn*engk'il, ools *ah*huwoom mury*ahth*ayoom, unoosura*n*uwoom w*ayn*um
Call in the coolies	kūlikkāre viḷikku	koolikk*ah*re wi*l*ikkoo
Muster them near the bungalow	avare veṅkḷāvinṟe samīpam viḷiccu kūṭṭi niṟttu	uware wengk*lah*winṯe sumeep'am wi*l*ichchŭ kootti n'iṟthoo
On account of the rain you have done only half a day's work	maṟa kāraṇam niṅṅaḷ pāti divasatte vēlayē ceytiṭṭuḷḷu	muṟu k*ah*ra*n*um ningngu*l* p*ah*th'i *th*iwasuththe w*ay*luy*ay* cheyth'ittoo*ll*oo
I did not see you in the working place	niṅṅaḷe paṇi-stalattȧ ñān kaṇṭillallō	ningngu*l*e pu*n*i-sthulaththŭ *nyah*n ku*n*t'illull*oh*
Take all the tools	ellā āyudaṅṅalum eṭukkuka	ell*ah* *ah*yoo*th*ungngu*l*oom et'ookkook'u
Go to the hill	kunnin-malekku pōkuka	koon'n'oommalekkŭ p*oh*k'ook'u
Each man must dig forty holes a day	ōrōruttanum divasam tōṟum nālpatu kuṛi vītam veṭṭaṇam	*oh*r*oh*rooththunoom *th*iwasum th*oh*ṟoom n'*ah*lp'uthŭ kooṛi weeth'am wettu*n*um
Do not pull up the plants	ceṭikaḷ paṟikkarutȧ	chet'ik'u*l* puṟikkuṟooth'ŭ
Mark the place where you must dig	nī kiḷakkēṇṭunna dikkȧ aṭayāḷappeṭuttuka	n'ee ki*l*akk*ayn*t'oon'n'u *th*ikkŭ ut'a*yahl*up-pet'ooththook'u
Trample the earth down	maṇṇȧ cavuṭṭi nikattuka	mu*nn*ŭ chuwootti nek'uththook'u

English.	Malayalam.	Pronunciation.
The dug-out earth is useless ; put in new earth only	kiḷac-ceṭutta maṇṇá koṇṭu upayōgam illa ; putiya maṇṇē iṭāvu	ki*l*ach-chet'ōōththu mu*nn*ŭ ko*n*t'ŭ ōōpuyo*h*gum illu ; pōōth'iyu mu*nnay* it'*ah*wōō
Go and fetch the plants from the nursery	ceṭippurayil pōyi, ceṭikaḷ eṭuttu koṇṭu varika	chet'ippōōrayil p*oh*yi chet'iku*l* et'ōōththŭ ko*n*t'ŭ wurik'u
Take up the plants with the earth	ceṭikaḷe (or taikkaḷe) maṇṇōṭu kūṭe paṟikkuka	chet'iku*l*e (*or* th*i*kku*l*e) mu*nnoh*t'ŭ koot'i puṟikkōōk'u

Changing Money (Paṇam māṟṟal)

Where can I get money changed ?	evite ninná enikku paṇam māṟṟi-k-kiṭṭum ?	evite n'in'n'ŭ enikkŭ pu*n*um m*ah*ṯṯi-k-kittōōm
Where is the bank (a money changer) ?	bāṅku (or uṇṭika) (paṇam māṟṟum stalam) eviṭe ?	b*ah*ŋgk'ŭ (*or* ōō*n*t'ik'u) (pu*n*um m*ah*ṯṯōōm sthulum) ewit'e
I want change for a five pound note	enikku oru añcupavan nōṭṭinná cillaṟa veṇam	enikkŭ orōō unych'ōō-puwun n*oh*ttinnŭ chillaṟu w*ay*-*n*um
Will you give me Indian money ?	enikku indyan paṇattil māṟṟam tarāmō ?	enikkŭ in'*th*yan pu*n*uththil m*ah*ṯṯam thur*ah*m*oh*
What is the exchange on English money ?	iṅkḷīṣu paṇavu-māyuḷḷa māṟṟa nirakku etṟa ?	iŋgk'*l*eeshŭ pu*n*uwōōm*ah*yōō*ll*u m*ah*ṯṯu n'irakkŭ ethṟu
Will you change me a sovereign ?	enikku oru pavan māṟṟi-t-tarāmō ?	enikkŭ orōō puwan m*ah*ṯṯi-th-thur*ah*-m*oh*

English.	Malayalam.	Pronunciation.
Will you cash this cheque for me ?	enikku ī cekku māṟ-ṟi-t-tarāmō ?	enikkŭ ee chekkŭ mahṯṯi-th-thurah-moh
Please give me gold and silver, not paper money	dayavu ceytȧ enik-ku svarṇa veḷḷi nāṇayaṅṅaḷ tari-ka ; nōṭṭukaḷ vēṇṭa	thuyawŭ cheyth'ŭ e-nikkŭ swuṟnu welli nahnayungngul thurik'u ; nohttoo-k'ul waynt'u
A bill of exchange	huṇṭiyal ; paṇam-māṟṟa billȧ	hoont'iyal ; punam-mahṯṯu billŭ
It is payable at sight	atȧ hājarākkum sa-mayattil koṭuk-kēṇṭatāṇȧ	uth'ŭ hahjarahk-koom sumayuth-thil kot'ookkayn-t'uth'ahnŭ
Give me the amount in rupees	saṃkhya uṟuppika-yāy tarika	sumkyu ooṟooppi-k'uyahy thurik'u

MONEY, WEIGHTS AND MEASURES.

Currency.

1. Malabar and Cochin.*

Copper. 1 pie = $\frac{1}{12}$ anna = $\frac{3}{32}$d.
3 pies = 1 mukkāl = $\frac{9}{32}$d.
6 pies = 1 half-anna = $\frac{9}{16}$d.
Nickel. 12 pies = 1 anna = 1$\frac{1}{8}$d.
2 annas = 2$\frac{1}{4}$d.
Silver and Nickel. 4 annas = 4$\frac{1}{2}$d.
8 annas = 1 half-rupee = 9d.
Silver and Paper. 16 annas = 1 Rupee = 1s. 6d.

Paper. 2$\frac{1}{2}$ Rupees = 3s. 9d.
5 Rupees = 7s. 6d.
10 Rupees = 15s.
50 Rupees = £3, 15s.
100 Rupees = £7, 10s.
500 Rupees = £37, 10s.
1000 Rupees = £75

2. Travancore.

16 kāsu = 1 cakṛam = $\frac{5}{8}$d.
28 cākṛam = 1 Travancore Rupee = 1s. 5$\frac{11}{16}$d.
28$\frac{1}{2}$ cākṛam = 1 (British) Rupee = 1s. 6d.

3. Used only for computation purposes.

Maḷabar. 2 pies = 1 kāsu = $\frac{1}{6}$d. (approx.).
4 pies = 1 paissa = $\frac{1}{3}$d. (approx.).
Cochin. 10 pies = 1 puttan = $\frac{5}{6}$d. (approx.).
5$\frac{1}{3}$ puttans = 1 paṇam = 4$\frac{7}{16}$d. (approx.).

1 Rupee = 1s. 6d. in English Money.
1 £ = 13$\frac{1}{3}$ Rupees in Indian money.
1 Rupee = 0$36c. in American money.†
1$ = Rs. 2-12as. in Indian money.

---

* The Currency of the Indian Government, available for use throughout India.

† At 4.86 $ to the £.

Weights.

	Troy.	Avoirdupois.
4 nenmaṇi = 1 kunnikkuru	1.5 to 2 grs (approx.)	
2 kunnikkuru = 1 mañcāṭi =	3 to 4.15 grs. ,,	
2 mañcāṭi = 1 paṇattūkkam =	6 grs. ,,	
10 paṇattūkkam = 1 kaṛiñcu =	60 grs.	
12 kaṛiñcu = 1 palam =	720 grs.	
4 palam = 1 ṛāttal =		1 lb.
25 ṛāttal = 1 tulām =		25 lb.
20 tulām = 1 bāram =		500 lbs.
28 tulām = 1 kaṇṭi =		700 lbs.

Linear Measure.

12 viral (finger-breadth) = 1 cāṇ (span).
2 cāṇ = 1 muṛam (cubit).
2 muṛam = 1 vāra (yard).
2 vāra = 1 daṇḍā (fathom).
2,000 daṇḍu = 1 kōśam = 2 Indian miles.

The term now in common use for an English mile is kallā (pron. kullŭ) (= *stone*), indicating the distance between two mile-stones.

Measure of Capacity.

2 āṛakkā = 1 uṛakkā.
2 uṛakkā = 1 uri.
2 uri = 1 naṛi.
4 naṛi = 1 iṭaṅgaṛi.
10 itaṅgaṛi = 1 paṛa.

POSTAL RATES.

The postal rate from India to the United Kingdom are as follows:—For letters from India, 2 annas per oz. Postcards, 1¼ annas per ounce. Newspapers, 1 anna per 50 grs.